Contents

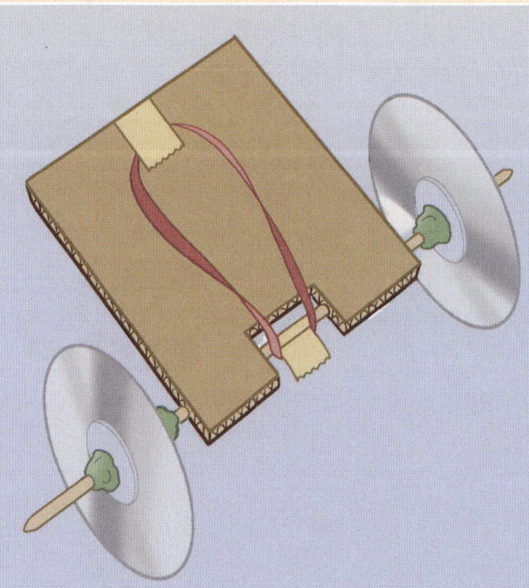

TARGETING SCIENCE YEAR 6 © PASCAL PRESS ISBN: 9781925726558

TARGETING SCIENCE YEAR 6 © PASCAL PRESS ISBN: 9781925726558

MY CONSTELLATION

Targeting Science Year 6

ISBN: 9781925726558

Published by Pascal Press
PO Box 250
Glebe NSW 2037
www.pascalpress.com.au
contact@pascalpress.com.au

This edition of *Skill Sharpeners: Science* is published by arrangement with Evan-Moor Corporation, USA.

For sale in Australia and New Zealand.

Authors: Guadalupe Lopez, Lisa Vitarisi Mathews
Publisher: Lynn Dickinson
Cover design: Janice Bowles
Illustrator: Paul Lennon, *www.dreamstime.com.au*
Editor Australian edition: Stella Tarakson
Typesetter: Stacey Grainger

Introduction

Welcome to your Year 6 *Targeting Science* activity book! It is packed with interesting and exciting activities to help you understand and enjoy science at home or school.

Targeting Science has been written to support the Australian Primary Science Curriculum Version 9.0 and is divided between:

- Biological Sciences
- Earth & Space Sciences
- Physical Sciences
- Chemical Sciences

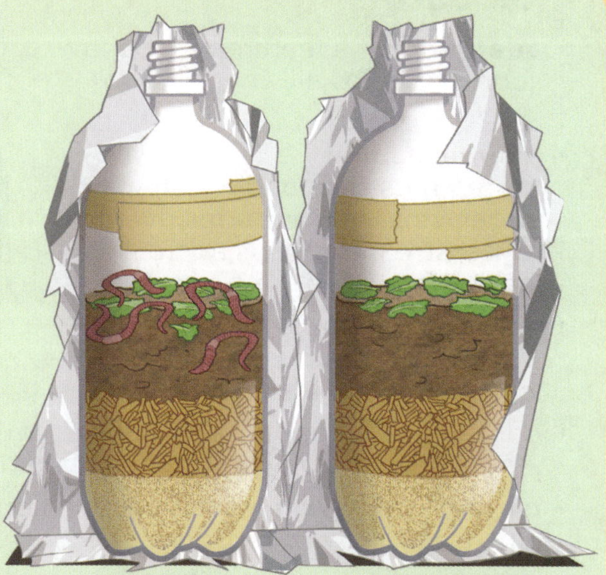

bottle with earthworms   bottle without earthworms

The Science Understanding and Inquiry Skills elements (including Science as a Human Endeavour) are embedded.

Hands-on activities provide opportunities to bring the science concepts to life. The exercises develop process skills such as observing, collecting, recording and organising information and making models of scientific events that happen in the natural world. All activities use easily sourced, inexpensive items.

Topics are introduced with explanations plus images to provide background information. Some lessons include a QR code where you can access a video for further explanations. You will be challenged to match, sort, label, sequence, analyse and answer questions with regular vocabulary practice puzzles throughout the book to help familiarise you with scientific terms. See the Glossary on the next page for some terms you may not already know. Answers are included at the end of the book.

FREE Teaching Guide.

This QR code links to a downloadable PDF of a Teaching Guide to support the material in this student workbook. The guide contains:

- Teaching plans and checklists.
- Graphic organisers.
- Material request forms (to send home for parents).
- Background information about each major topic as well as extension activities.

Use this QR code to access the FREE Teaching Guide.

Front cover – have you looked at the front cover? It depicts what life was like before a significant scientific discovery that led to the development of new technology. What is the difference between Science and Technology? The following quote sums it up nicely.

Science is the process of acquiring knowledge of natural phenomenon along with various reasons. Technology is the application of Science to the solution of problems. (Sismondo, 2018)

Glossary

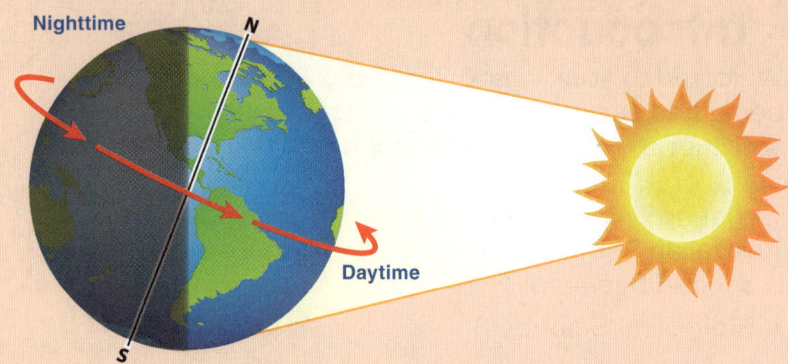

- **adaptation** – a feature or a behaviour that helps a living thing to survive.
- **aquatic habitat** – a habitat with water in its surroundings in which organisms live – includes rivers, lakes, streams, ponds and other bodies of water.
- **conductors** - materials through which heat, sound or electrical energy are freely transferred.
- **coral reef** – an underwater ecosystem populated by reef-building corals. Reefs are formed of colonies of coral polyps held together by calcium carbonate.
- **current** – a flowing movement in a liquid, gas, plasma or other form of matter, especially one that follows a recognisable course. A flow of positive electric charge.
- **ecosystem** – a community or group of living organisms that live in and interact with each other in a specific environment.
- **electrical circuit** – a conducting loop of wire and an energy source like a battery that allows electric current to flow around.
- **electrons** – negatively charged particles in an atom.
- **environment** - all the surroundings, living and non-living.
- **escape velocity** – the minimum velocity with which an object can escape the gravitational pull of a planet.
- **gravity** – the invisible force of attraction between any two objects. The force by which a planet or other body draws objects towards its centre.
- **habitat** - the natural environment of an organism such as a plant or animal.
- **Insulators** - materials which inhibit the transfer of heat, sound or electrical energy.
- **irreversible changes** – when something cannot be changed back to its original form. In many irreversible changes, new materials and substances may be formed.
- **lightning** – a giant spark of electricity in the atmosphere between clouds, the air, or the ground.
- **parallel circuit** – an electrical path that branches so that the current divides and only part of it flows through any branch.
- **resistors** – a device having resistance to an electrical current.
- **reversible change** – a change that can be undone or reversed.
- **revolving** – move in a circle on a central axis.
- **series circuit** - circuit elements are arrange in a single path along which the whole current flows to each component.
- **terrestrial habitat** – habitats found on land like forests, grasslands, deserts, shorelines and wetlands. Also include man-made habitats like farms, towns, cities and underground caves and mines.

SAFETY
All of the investigations in this book are designed for kids to do safely in the home or classroom. However, adult supervision is recommended.

TARGETING SCIENCE YEAR 6 © PASCAL PRESS ISBN: 9781925726558

Year 6 Australian Science Curriculum Correlations

ACARA Code	Content description	Strand	Sub strand	Pages
AC9S6U01	Investigate the physical conditions of a habitat and analyse how the growth and survival of living things is affected by changing physical conditions.	Science Understanding	Biological Sciences	2-16
AC9S6U02	Describe the movement of Earth and other planets relative to the sun and model how Earth's tilt, rotation on its axis and revolution around the sun relate to cyclic observable phenomena, including variable day and night length.	Science Understanding	Earth & Space Sciences	17-72
AC9S6U03	Investigate the transfer and transformation of energy in electrical circuits, including the role of circuit components, insulators and conductors.	Science Understanding	Physical Sciences	73-105
AC9S6U04	Compare reversible changes, including dissolving and changes of state, and irreversible changes, including cooking and rusting that produce new substances.	Science Understanding	Chemical Sciences	106-138
AC9S6H01	Examine why advances in science are often the result of collaboration or build on the work of others.	Science as Human Endeavour	Nature and Development of Science	11, 12, 14, 60, 123
AC9S6H02	Investigate how scientific knowledge is used by individuals and communities to identify problems, consider responses and make decisions.	Science as Human Endeavour	Use and Influence of Science	10, 14, 61, 122
AC9S6I01	Pose investigable questions to identify patterns and test relationships and make reasoned predictions.	Science Inquiry	Questioning and Predicting	7, 8, 13, 21, 111, 115, 136
AC9S6I02	Plan and conduct repeatable investigations to answer questions including, as appropriate, deciding the variables to be changed, measured and controlled in fair tests; describing potential risks; planning for the safe use of equipment and materials; and identifying required permissions to conduct investigations on Country/Place.	Science Inquiry	Planning and Conducting	7, 13, 21, 22, 56, 63, 70, 84, 86, 103, 111, 115, 120, 136
AC9S6I03	Use equipment to observe, measure and record data with reasonable precision, using digital tools as appropriate.	Science Inquiry	Planning and Conducting	7, 13, 21, 27, 112, 118, 136
AC9S6I04	Construct and use appropriate representations, including tables, graphs and visual or physical models, to organise and process data and information and describe patterns, trends and relationships.	Science Inquiry	Processing, Modelling and Analysing	5, 7, 13, 16, 20, 25, 26, 30, 31, 32, 38, 44, 46, 49, 50, 52, 54, 57, 61, 66, 68, 75, 76, 89, 108, 112, 129, 132
AC9S6I05	Compare methods and findings with those of others, recognise possible sources of error, pose questions for further investigation and select evidence to draw reasoned conclusions.	Science Inquiry	Evaluating	7, 13, 21, 56, 57, 64, 85, 86, 112, 117, 119, 137
AC9S6I06	Write and create texts to communicate ideas and findings for specific purposes and audiences, including selection of language features, using digital tools as appropriate.	Science Inquiry	Communicating	7, 8, 9, 13, 21, 33, 46, 53, 54, 64, 67, 71, 80, 96, 100, 109, 121, 132

Plants Need Water

Concepts:

Some plants get water through their roots.

Define It!

absorb: to take in or soak up

nonvascular: having no tissues or vessels to carry water or nutrients

vascular: having tissues that are able to transport water and nutrients

Every living thing—people, animals, and plants—needs water in order to grow and survive. Plants usually get water from rainfall that soaks into the ground. They take in the water through their roots. Plants with roots, stems, and leaves such as trees and flowers are called **vascular** plants. The roots of a vascular plant **absorb** water from the soil and move it into the stems and leaves.

Some plants, called **nonvascular** plants, absorb water and nutrients from their surroundings. Nonvascular plants such as moss do not have true roots, stems, or leaves with tubes for moving water throughout the plant. Instead, water passes directly from cell to cell. Because of this, nonvascular plants do not grow very tall.

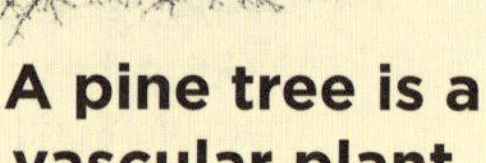

A pine tree is a vascular plant.

Moss is a nonvascular plant.

Complete each sentence.

1. The roots of a vascular plant ____

   ____.

2. Nonvascular plants do not have ______________________________ or leaves.

TARGETING SCIENCE YEAR 6 © PASCAL PRESS ISBN: 9781925726558

Plants Need Sunlight and CO_2

Plants make their own food using water, sunlight, and carbon dioxide (CO_2). These ingredients create the nutrients they need to **sustain** life.

Plants absorb sunlight and carbon dioxide through their leaves. Cells in the leaves called **chloroplasts** contain the chemical **chlorophyll**. Chlorophyll is a green pigment that attracts light energy. It allows plant cells to absorb sunlight and **convert** it into energy. It also gives plants their green colour. Carbon dioxide in the air enters the plant cells through tiny pores called **stomata**, which are located on the underside of leaves.

Define It!

chlorophyll: a green pigment in plants that absorbs sunlight

chloroplasts: cells that contain chlorophyll and convert sunlight into energy

convert: to change in form

stomata: tiny pores that allow gases to move in and out of a plant

sustain: to provide what is needed to exist or continue

Inside a Leaf

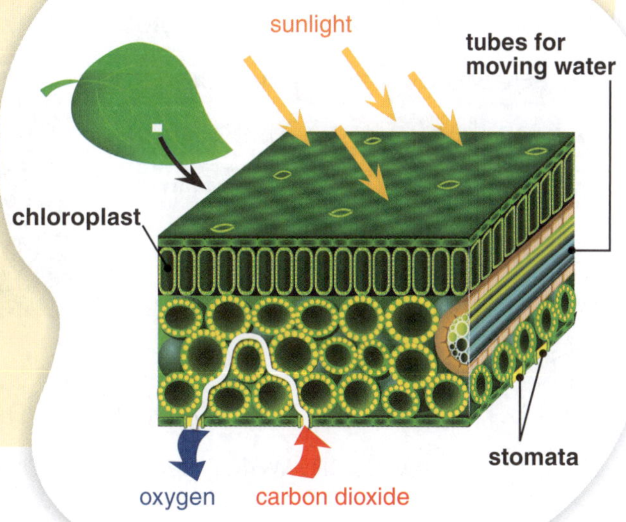

Concepts: Plants make their own food using sunlight, water, and CO_2.

Answer the questions.

1. Which chemical allows plants to absorb sunlight? Where is it located?

____

2. Through which parts does carbon dioxide enter the plant? Where are they located?

____

Survival

Photosynthesis

Concepts:

Plants make their own food through photosynthesis.

Define It!

photosynthesis: the process by which plants use sunlight, carbon dioxide, and water to create food

transpiration: the passage of water vapour through a plant's pores

Plants are able to create their own food in a process called **photosynthesis**. During photosynthesis, sunlight is combined with water and carbon dioxide (CO_2). This process changes the CO_2, water, and sunlight into energy, which becomes food for the plant.

What happens after plants use the food energy they create? Just like animals, plants produce waste. The waste is stored in cells until it can be removed. During photosynthesis, water molecules are separated into hydrogen and oxygen. Hydrogen is used to create energy. Oxygen becomes waste and is expelled through the stomata. Some water that is absorbed by plants also becomes waste. This water moves out of plants in a process called **transpiration**. During transpiration, water passes through the stomata and becomes water vapour in the air.

Write *true* or *false*.

1. Plants do not produce waste. __________
2. Plants convert water, sunlight, and CO_2 into food energy. __________
3. Oxygen and water are waste products of plants. __________
4. Plants make food in a process called transpiration. __________

TARGETING SCIENCE YEAR 6 © PASCAL PRESS ISBN: 9781925726558

Skills:

Interpret and identify information in graphic representations.

This diagram of a plant shows what a plant takes in during photosynthesis and what it expels.

1. Label the three ingredients plants need to make food.

2. Label the two waste products plants produce.

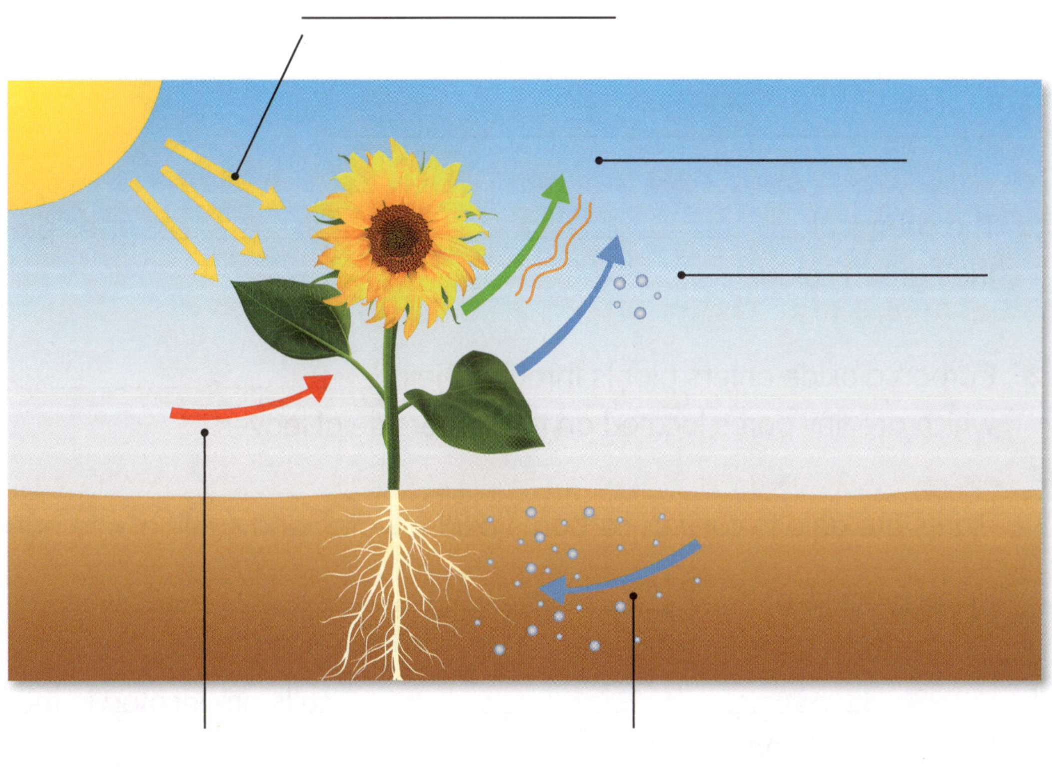

3. Describe how the plant absorbs the ingredients and gets rid of its waste. Include as much detail as you can.

Survival

Vocabulary Practic

Skill: Apply content vocabulary.

Select from the list of vocabulary words to complete the sentences. Then unscramble the shaded letters to decode the secret message. **Hint:** Look at the picture if you need help decoding the message.

nonvascular	absorb	photosynthesis	transpiration
chlorophyll	stomata	chloroplast	vascular

1. Plants with stems such as flowers are ___ ___ ___ ___ ___ ___ ___ ___, and plants without stems such as moss are ___ ___ ___ ___ ___ ___ ___ ___ ___ ___ ___.

2. The chemical ___ ___ ___ ___ ___ ___ ___ ___ ___ ___ ___ gives plants their green colour.

3. Carbon dioxide enters plants through their ___ ___ ___ ___ ___ ___ ___, which are tiny pores located on the underside of leaves.

4. Plants are able to convert carbon dioxide, water, and sunlight into nutrients in the process of ___ ___ ___ ___ ___ ___ ___ ___ ___ ___ ___ ___ ___ ___.

5. ___ ___ ___ ___ ___ ___ ___ ___ ___ ___ ___ cells are located in the plant's leaves and absorb sunlight.

6. Vascular plants ___ ___ ___ ___ ___ ___ water through their roots.

___ ___ ___ ___ ___ ___ ___ ___ is a type of moss that can grow in arctic, mild, forest, and desert regions.

Survival

TARGETING SCIENCE YEAR 6 © PASCAL PRESS ISBN: 9781925726558

Take It or Leaf It

These two experiments demonstrate how sunlight and carbon dioxide affect the process of photosynthesis.

What You Need

- 2 potted plants of the same age and species
- petroleum jelly

Skills:

Conduct experiments, make observations, and analyse data.

Directions

1. Write "control" on one pot and "PJ" (for petroleum jelly) on the other pot.
2. Wipe petroleum jelly on the PJ plant's leaves. Be sure to completely cover every leaf with jelly.
3. Place both plants next to a window that gets a lot of sunlight for four weeks. Give each plant about ½ cup (120 mL) of water every other day. Record your observations.

Record your observations in the table. Then answer the questions below.

	CONTROL				PJ			
	WEEK 1	WEEK 2	WEEK 3	WEEK 4	WEEK 1	WEEK 2	WEEK 3	WEEK 4
Number of new leaves growing								
Height of plant								
Width of plant								
Overall health of plant, scale of 1 to 10								

1. Compare the plant covered in petroleum jelly to the control plant. How was the growth of the two plants different from one another?

____

____

2. Why do you think covering a plant's leaves in petroleum jelly would change how the plant grows?

____

Survival

Plant Maze

Skills:

Conduct experiments, make observations, and analyse data.

What You Need

- shoebox with lid
- cardboard
- scissors
- tape
- small beansprout plant (in plastic cup with soil)

Directions

1. Cut a large hole at one end of the shoebox. Use tape to cover any areas of the shoebox where light might shine through.
2. Cut two pieces of cardboard that measure the same height as the shoebox and half of its width.
3. Tape one piece of cardboard on the left-hand side of the box as shown. Tape the second piece on the right-hand side as shown.
4. Stand the shoebox on end with the hole on top. Place the beansprout in the shoebox as shown. Make sure the plant has been well watered.
5. Close the box, tape it shut, and place it on a sunny windowsill.
6. In about 4 or 5 days, open the box. Record your observations of the way the plant grew.

What Did You Discover?

1. In what direction did the beansprout grow? Why do you think it grew that way?

____

____

2. What do you think would have happened if you had cut a hole in the side of the box instead of the top?

____

3. What do you think would have happened if you had not allowed any sunlight into the box?

____

Survival

TARGETING SCIENCE YEAR 6 © PASCAL PRESS ISBN: 9781925726558

Picking Favourites

Imagine that the sun, carbon dioxide, and water are having an argument about who is most important in the process of photosynthesis. Pretend you are the plant listening to their argument. Write a story about the argument. Tell the sun, CO_2, and water why they are important to photosynthesis.

Skill:

Write narratives to develop real or imagined experiences or events.

Survival

Changes to Conditions

A **habitat** is a place or area within an **environment** where a living thing is able to meet its needs. A habitat is always an environment, but an environment is not always a habitat. A habitat always has life in it, whereas the environment does not necessarily have life in it.

An **adaptation** is any passed on trait that helps an organism, such as a plant or animal, survive and reproduce in its environment.

If something changes in an environment or habitat, living things within that environment are affected. These changes can be rapid (such as a flood or fire) or gradual, such as a change to the climate over a longer period of time.

Rapid change example:

If a pond with aquatic plants, fish, frogs, dragonflies and mosquitoes experiences a dramatic change in rainfall or temperatures such as a drought, everything within that environment has to adapt or change, or it dies.

1. Think about the things that would happen if the water dried up. Which life cycles would be most affected?

___

Gradual change example:

Corroboree Frogs are one of the most critically endangered species in Australia. Disease, habitat loss, feral animals and changing climate conditions have meant that, over time, numbers have become dangerously low in the wild.

2. What will happen if these things are not changed or controlled? Why?

___

Did you know that Taronga Park Zoo in Sydney has been working tirelessly to save these frogs from extinction? They have bred and released hundreds of frogs and thousands of eggs back into the wild, and environmental scientists are working hard to improve their natural habitats and remove these threats.

Changing Conditions

Naturally occurring **terrestrial habitats** are found on land, like forests, grasslands, deserts, shorelines, and wetlands.

Naturally occurring **aquatic habitats** are found in and around bodies of water, like lakes, rivers, ponds, and wetlands.

An **ecosystem** is made up of all the living organisms in an area (plants and animals) and all of the non-living organisms (water, dirt, rocks).

Habitats are directly affected by natural and man-made changes. The amount of rainfall and temperature in an area impacts the type of animals and plants that can live there. The actions of humans and other animal species also directly affect a habitat and the life within it.

Think through these scenarios, and how each change might affect the habitat and living things within it. Some impacts might be positive and some may be negative. The first three are done for you as examples.

Habitat:	Change:	Impact on plants:	Impact on animals:	Impact on non-living elements:
A lake	Large amount of rainfall.	Some plants on the edge of the lake may be submerged and die. Aquatic plants may grow and spread further.	Frogs, insects and other aquatic animals will thrive and reproduce. Land dwelling animals close to waters edge may need to relocate.	Erosion could occur and flooding could cause damage to surrounding landscapes.
A shallow creek	Cattle using the creek for water.	Plants crushed by cattle feet. Weeds brought in on cattle hooves.	Aquatic animals have less water to breed and grow. Water made muddy and less suitable for life. Cows leave waste in creek which changes water quality and brings disease.	Less water in the creek. Rocks and soil disturbed and more prone to erosion.
a desert environment	Feral cats increase in numbers.	Little effect on plants.	Huge numbers of native animals killed by cats, therefore unable to reproduce. Decline in populations.	Little effect on non-living elements.
A beach	Oil spill washes up onto beach.			
A native forest	A new housing estate is started.			

The Case for Coral

https://clickv.ie/w/Qzgx

Use this QR code to access a video on this topic.

A **coral reef** is a living thing found in the warmer waters across our planet. A large coral reef is one of nature's most beautiful treasures. The Great Barrier Reef is in the Coral Sea, on Australia's north-eastern coast. It is the largest living organism on Earth and the only living thing the naked eye can see from space! It's not made up of a single reef but nearly 3000 smaller ones.

Coral is an animal. They glue their tiny skeletons to a rock and stay in the same place for their whole lives. The problem is that coral is very sensitive to light and temperature changes and the depth of the water above it. If the sea water becomes too hot, sea levels too high, or the water becomes too polluted, the coral can die. Severe storms and cyclones can also damage coral.

Coral bleaching happens when coral reefs are under too much stress. They eject the algae living on them and turn completely white. This doesn't always mean the coral is dead, but they become more vulnerable to death, especially if the stress continues for a long period of time.

In recent years, scientists have developed instruments for measuring the health of coral in an attempt to try to come up with solutions for the future.

True or False?

Coral is a plant.	Coral bleaching only happens to stressed coral.	Coral moves from place to place.
Coral grows in warmer waters.	You can see the Great Barrier Reef from space.	Coral is living.
Coral ejects algae from its body when it is stressed.	Coral is not affected by the height of the water above it.	The Great Barrier Reef is made up of 3000 smaller reefs.

TARGETING SCIENCE YEAR 6 © PASCAL PRESS ISBN: 9781925726558

Mouldy Bread

Ever opened the bread bag to find a nasty, mouldy surprise? Why did the mould grow on the bread? Could you have stopped it from growing?

https://clickv.ie/w/wxgx

Use this QR code to access a video on this topic.

Try this experiment to test the growth of mould on bread in different positions.

Take three slices of the same type of bread and spray them lightly with the same amount of water. Place each one in a sealed zip-lock bag. Put them each in a different position, for example one in a sunny corner, one in the dark and one in the fridge.

1. Come up with a focus question: What are you trying to find out?

____

2. Control your variables to make it a fair test:

What is the one variable you are going to change?	What is the one thing you are going to measure or observe?	What are three things you will need to keep the same?

3. Check each slice of bread every day for up to 10 days. Fill in this data table as you go.

AT NO STAGE - EVEN WHEN THE EXPERIMENT IS OVER - SHOULD YOU OPEN THE BAGS. ALWAYS MAKE YOUR OBSERVATIONS THROUGH THE OUTSIDE OF THE BAG.

	DAY 1	DAY 2	DAY 3	DAY 4	DAY 5	DAY 6	DAY 7	DAY 8	DAY 9	DAY 10
BAG 1: ______										
BAG 2: ______										
BAG 3: ______										

4. What did you observe from this experiment after the 10 days and why do you think this happened?

____

5. Does this experiment change the place you might like to store your bread to prevent mould? Why?

____

Lights Out for Birds

The amount of artificial light on the Earth's surface is increasing by at least two percent each year, contributing to the death of millions of migrating birds. Many birds migrate in darkness, and use the stars in the night sky to navigate. When they are faced with artificial light and reflections from tall buildings, they can lose their way, or, worse still, crash into things.

These two pictures show the night sky a bird would see when there is no artificial light, compared to when there is artificial light.

When there is too much light in an area, or there is a change in the type or amount of lighting, it can impact on when the birds migrate and other behaviours.

Many countries now realise that natural darkness has to be conserved for the good of the wildlife on our planet, just as we need to protect clean water, air and soil. Governments are taking measures such as:

Red-necked Stints are the size and weight of a matchbox, yet fly thousands of kilometres to nest in the Siberian tundra, before turning around six months later to migrate south to Australia once again.

- Installing downwards facing sources of artificial light to avoid light spill-over from street etc.
- Using dark-coloured surfaces that don't reflect light.
- Using lights with reduced or filtered harmful wavelengths.
- Using adaptive light controls to manage light timing, intensity and colour.

Even around our homes, there are things we can do to protect wildlife and help preserve a more natural environment. Can you think of ways you could make your home more mindful of wildlife at night? Draw your ideas in these boxes.

Migration and Hibernation - A First Nations Perspective

For millions of years, Australian First Nations people have been using their knowledge of weather patterns, life cycles and plant and animal behaviour to predict and sustainably draw on the resources from their country as well as understand weather patterns.

This knowledge is passed down from generation to generation through storytelling, art and demonstration. Now, more than ever, in the wake of the recent fires and catastrophic weather events, their perspectives are being drawn upon for guidance into land management practices. Their deep understanding of their country enables them to be sensitive to their local environment and help predict changes.

Some examples of their sensitivity to the nature in their surroundings are:

1. To the Yanyuwa people (Coastal,NT) rolling coastal clouds indicate that flying foxes and certain bird species are about to start their seasonal migration.
2. To the Wardaman people (WA) the appearance of march-flies in September or October indicate the end of the dry season.
3. To the Walabunnba people (South-west, NT) when the mirrlarr (rain bird) calls out, it indicates that there will be a lot of rain.
4. During the Djilba season in Nyoongar country (South-west, WA), the flowers of the balgas (grass trees) emerge in preparation for the coming Kambarang season.
5. The flowering of the boo'kerrikin (Acacia decurrens) is an indication for the D'harawal people (Sydney, NSW), an end to the cold, windy weather, and the beginning of the gentle spring rains.

Migration and Hibernation - A First Nations Perspective

The Ngan'gi people from the Daly River, Northern Territory, rely on the life cycle of spear grass to alert them to a change in season, and the best time to look for bush tucker. When the grass stalks die and turn a reddish colour as the dry season approaches, it's time to look for prawns in creeks. When the grass seeds turn brown and start falling, the dry season has started and it's time to fish for barramundi. When the grass has burnt, the turtles are fat and ideal to hunt.

Below is a seasonal calendar created from Miriwoong Country in the East Kimberley, WA. It shows the varying seasons and months divided between cold, wet and hot.

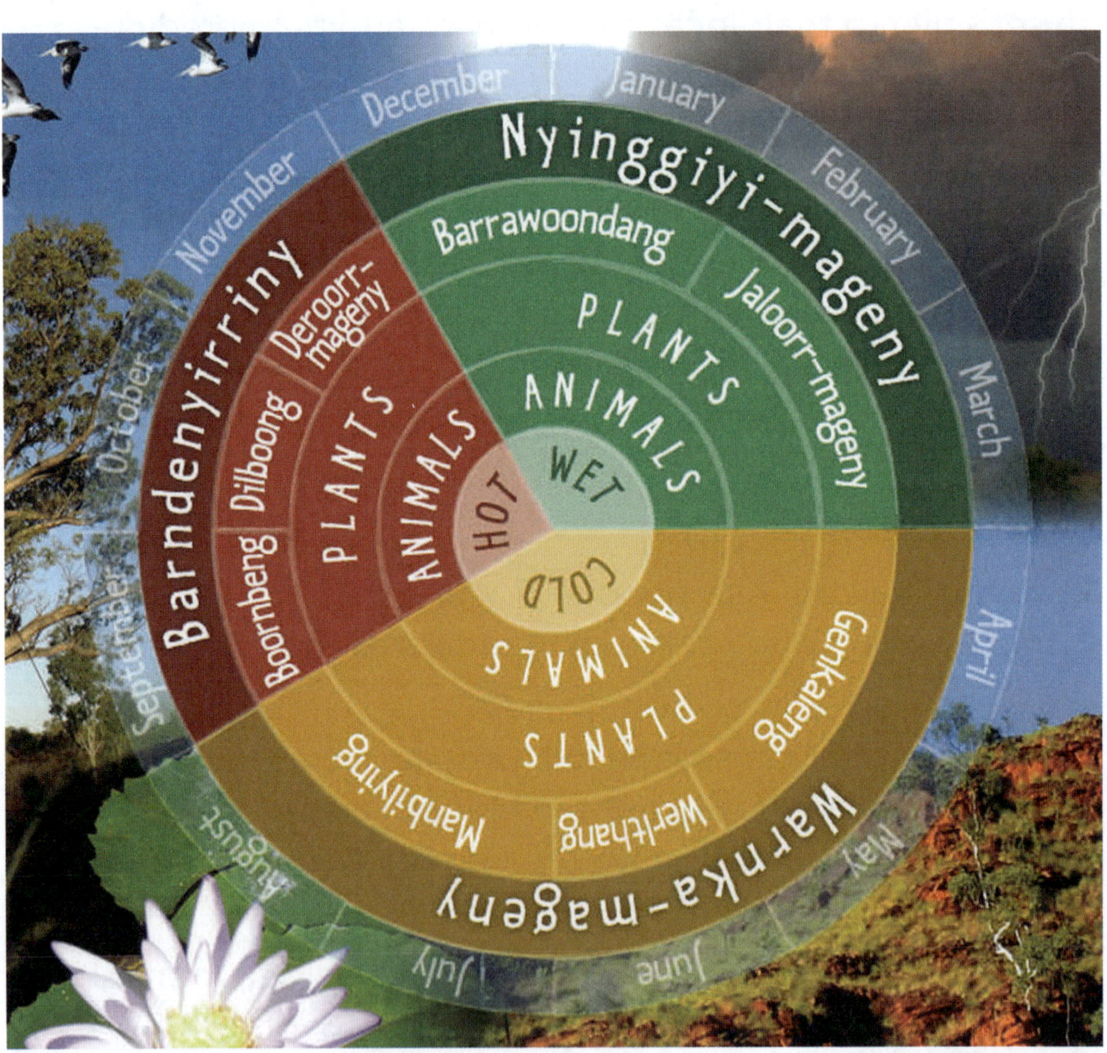

From Blake's Learning Centres: History Centres, Lower Primary, Blake Education. Used by permission of Mirima Dawang Woorlab-gerring Language and Culture Centre, www.mirima.org.au

TARGETING SCIENCE YEAR 6 © PASCAL PRESS ISBN: 9781925726558

Concepts:

Earth completes a single rotation in 24 hours.

As Earth spins, different parts of the planet receive sunlight.

Define It!

axis: an imaginary line that passes through the centre of Earth from the North Pole to the South Pole

rotate: to move or turn in a circle

Although we cannot feel its motion, Earth is constantly **rotating**. It spins around on its **axis**, an imaginary line that runs from the North Pole to the South Pole. It takes Earth 24 hours to make one rotation. That's why a single day is 24 hours long.

Earth rotates in an anticlockwise direction. Because of this, the sun appears to move through our sky from east to west. However, the sun is not moving—Earth is. As Earth spins, different parts of the planet receive sunlight. This causes Earth to have daytime on one side of the world while it is nighttime on the other side.

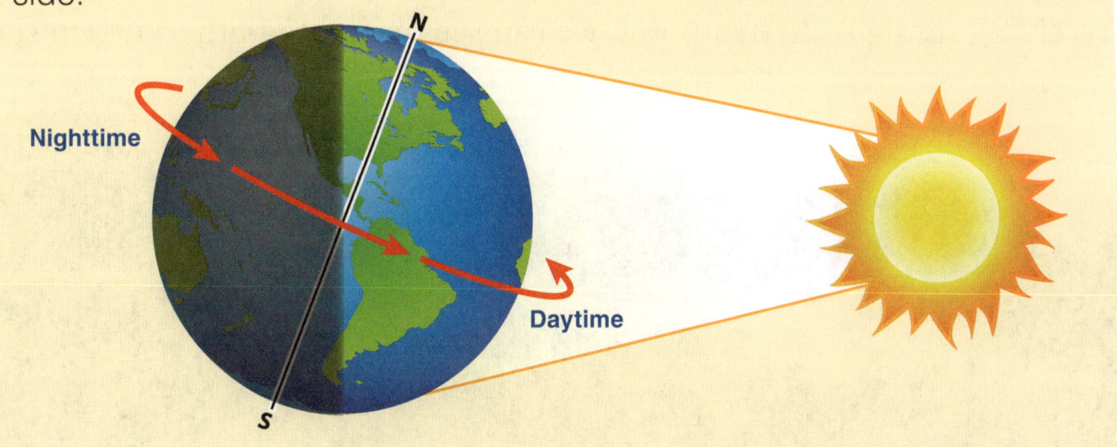

Answer the questions.

1. How many hours does it take for Earth to complete a rotation? ______________________

2. In which direction does Earth rotate? ______________________

3. Earth's axis passes between which two points? ______________________

TARGETING SCIENCE YEAR 6 © PASCAL PRESS ISBN: 9781925726558

Sunrise and Sunset

Concepts:

Stars do not move in the sky—it is Earth that rotates.

Because the sun is much closer to Earth than other stars, its light is brightest in our daytime sky.

Define It!

horizon: the line where the sky and Earth appear to meet

https://clickv.ie/w/jygx

Use this QR code to access a video on this topic.

The sun seems to rise over the eastern **horizon** to start each day. However, it is really Earth that moves. As Earth rotates toward the sun, the sun's rays light the sky. This makes the stars seem to disappear. Yet, the stars have not moved. You just can't see them because the light of the sun is much brighter than the faint light of the stars. This is not because our sun is larger or more powerful than other stars—it's because the sun is much closer to Earth than any other star is.

The sun appears to set in the west, but in reality, Earth is rotating away from the sun. After dusk, the light in the sky dims. After the sun has disappeared below the horizon, that side of the planet is no longer receiving sunlight. At that point, we can see the light of other distant stars.

Write *true* or *false*.

1. Earth rotates away from the stars during the day. ____________
2. The sun is the closest star to our planet. ____________
3. The sun sets on the western horizon. ____________
4. The light of the stars is only visible to us during the day. ____________

TARGETING SCIENCE YEAR 6 © PASCAL PRESS ISBN: 9781925726558

Daylight Hours Affect Temperature

Concept:

Earth's rotation regulates temperature, making it possible for life as we know it to exist.

If Earth were to stop rotating, life as we know it would be radically changed. It would take an entire year for Earth to experience one full cycle of light and darkness. That means we would have six months of day followed by six months of night!

The rotation of Earth **regulates** its temperature, allowing the planet to heat and cool evenly as it turns. If Earth stopped spinning, one **hemisphere** would **endure** extremely hot temperatures during the six full months of daylight. The hemisphere pointed away from the sun would experience six months of frigid temperatures and darkness. Plant and animal life that could not adapt to these harsh conditions would likely die.

Define It!

endure: to experience a hardship for a long time

hemisphere: half of Earth

regulate: to bring something under control

6 months of daytime

6 months of nighttime

Describe three things that would happen if Earth were to stop rotating.

1. ____

____

2. ____

____

3. ____

____

TARGETING SCIENCE YEAR 6 © PASCAL PRESS ISBN: 9781925726558

Hours of Daylight

Skill:

Interpret information from a graph or chart.

Over the course of one year, every place on Earth gets the same amount of daylight. But when the light comes to us and for how long differs by location and time of year. At the North and South Poles, the sun rises and sets only once each year. Six months of daylight are followed by six months of darkness.

It is much different at the equator. The amount of daylight does not change much throughout the year. Within each 24-hour period, there are about 12 hours of daylight and 12 hours of darkness.

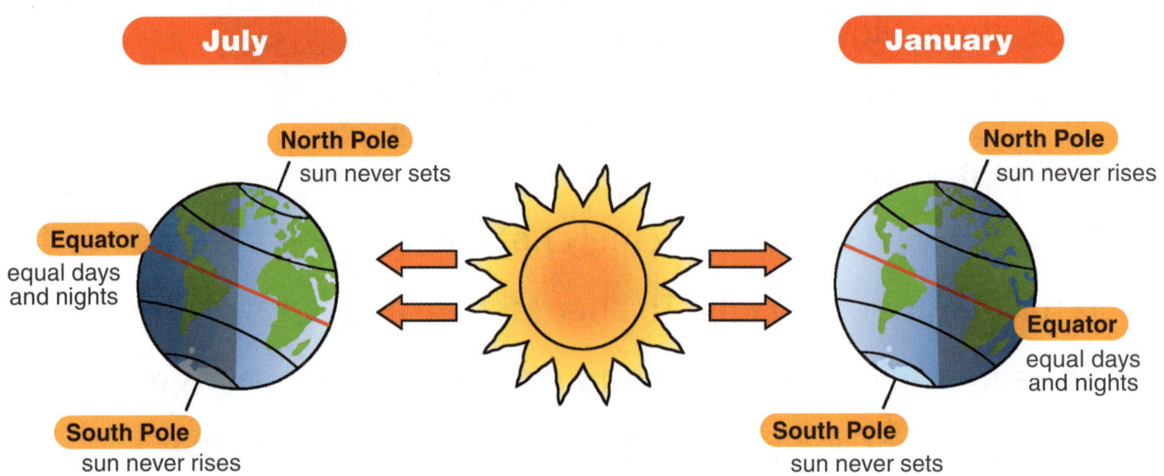

This chart shows the amount of daylight that four cities get in January and July. Use the information to list the cities in order of their distance from the North Pole.

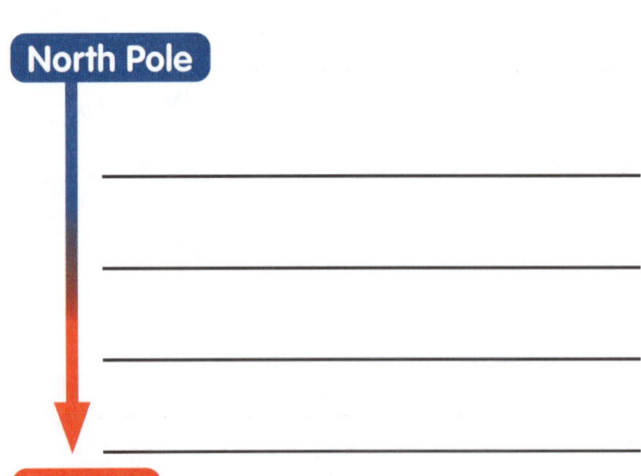

City	Hours of Daylight	
	January	July
Shanghai, China	10	14
Barrow, Alaska, U.S.	0	24
Bogota, Colombia	12	12
St. Petersburg, Russia	6	18

Space Perspectives

TARGETING SCIENCE YEAR 6 © PASCAL PRESS ISBN: 9781925726558

Earth's Rotation - Hands on Activity

Try this simple activity to see how the sun changes position in the sky as Earth rotates.

What You Need

- an area of concrete, such as a footpath
- chalk
- a partner
- measuring tape

Directions

1. In the morning, stand on the concrete with the sun behind you. Look for your shadow.
2. Use chalk to mark the place where you are standing. Have your partner mark the place where your shadow ends.
3. Draw a line to connect the two marks.
4. In the afternoon, go back to the same place. Stand on your first mark. Have your partner mark where your shadow ends now.

What Did You Discover?

1. In what direction did the first shadow point? In what direction did the second shadow point?

   ____

2. Did the shadows point in the same direction? ____________________

3. Measure the length of both shadows. Write the measurements.

   ____

4. Were the shadows the same length? ____________________

5. What do the lengths and directions of the shadows tell you about the position of the sun?

   ____

   ____

Skills: Conduct experi- ments and draw conclusions about the results.

Earth's Rotation - Hands on Activity

Try this simple activity to demonstrate how Earth's rotation creates the day and night cycle.

What You Need

- sticky note
- lamp with 200 watt bulb, and shade removed

Directions

1. Draw an X on the sticky note and label it with the name of your town. Place the note on your chest. The note represents the location of your town, and you represent Earth.
2. Go to a dark room and turn on the lamp. The lamp represents the sun.
3. Stand with your back to the lamp and your arms stretched out. Notice where the light of the lamp shines.
4. Rotate anticlockwise toward the lamp. Stop when your left arm is pointed toward the lamp. Notice where the light of the lamp shines.
5. Continue to rotate anticlockwise until you are facing the lamp. Notice where the light of the lamp shines.
6. Complete the rotation so that your back is to the lamp once again.

What Did You Discover?

1. What time of day was it in your town when you faced away from the lamp? ____________________
2. What time was it—sunrise or sunset—when your left arm pointed to the lamp? What time was it when your right arm pointed to the lamp? ____________________
3. About what time was it when you faced the lamp straight on? ____________________

TARGETING SCIENCE YEAR 6 © PASCAL PRESS ISBN: 9781925726558

Because of the Earth's rotation, different part of the world experience day and night at different moments. All countries use standard time zones to measure the time. Earth is divided into 24 time zones—one for each hour of the day. All time zones are calculated by the time, plus or minus, from GMT (Greenwich Mean Time). Greenwich, in the United Kingdom, sits on the Prime Meridien (0 degrees longitude), so all other time is measured by how far it is behind or in front of the Prime Meridien. For example, Queensland is 10 hours later than the time at Greenwich, GMT+10.

This map shows the time zones of Australia. Use the map to answer the questions below.

Skill: Interpret information from maps.

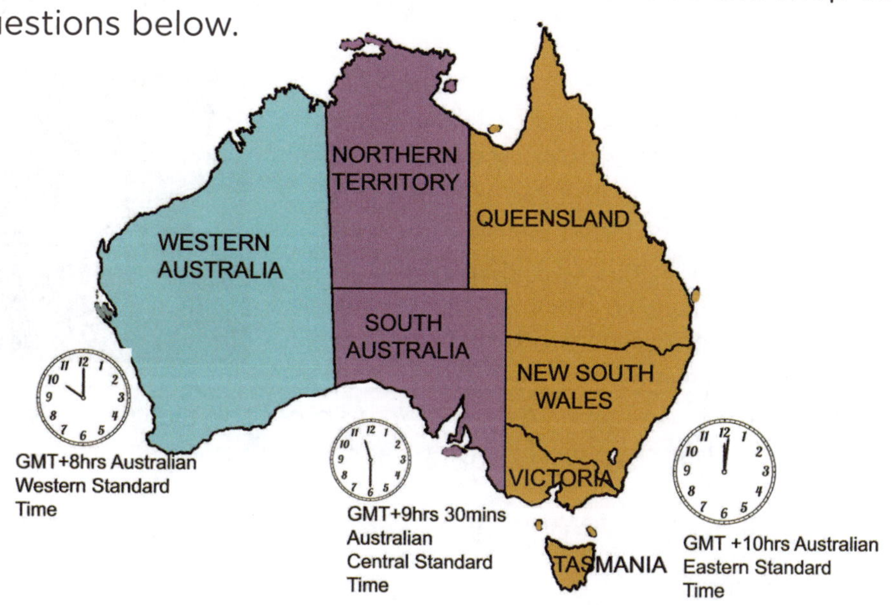

1. Australia is divided into how many standard time zones?

____

2. What is the time difference between each neighbouring time zone? ________________________

3. What time zone in Australia will see the sun come up first? ________________________

4. If it is 1pm in Sydney, NSW, what time is it in Perth, WA?

____

Daylight Saving: In Australia the clocks are put forward an hour between October and April in every state except Queensland and the Northern Territory.

5. My birthday is November 5 and I live in Adelaide, SA. I want to ring my grandparents to thank them for my present. If it is 9am at my house, what time will it be where they live in Queensland? ________________________

Gravity in Space

Gravity is the force that pulls us towards the centre of the Earth. If there was no gravity, we would all just float off into space.

Gravity doesn't only exist on Earth, it plays a role in the whole universe. It's because of gravity that each planet in our solar system orbits the sun. The gravitational pull of the sun keeps each planet **revolving** around it. The more mass something has, the greater its gravitational pull is on other objects. The bigger the object the more pull it has. The more distance there is between two objects, the less pull they have on each other. The relationship between our moon and the Earth is due to the pull from our planet. There is gravity on the moon, but it is six times less than it is on Earth.

For a spacecraft to leave Earth, it must have an enormous **escape velocity** (speed out to space) to be able to pull away from the gravity on Earth. As it gets nearer to the moon, it will have more pull towards the moon and less from Earth.

Even though the moon has less gravitational pull than the Earth, it is still able to have some influence on us. Ever wondered why we have high and low tides? It is because the pull of the moon causes the oceans near it to bulge towards it. As the earth spins, the bulge moves, pulling the water to higher and lower points across the planet.

1. What is the invisible force that pulls us towards the centre of the Earth called? ______________
2. What would happen if there was no gravity on the Earth?

   ____
3. What two words best describe what affects the strength of a gravitational pull?

   ____
4. What is the main affect of the moon's gravitational pull on Earth?

   ____
5. Would there more more or less gravity between two objects in space if they were further apart? ________________________
6. Would planets smaller than Earth have a greater or lesser gravitational pull?________________
7. If there was no gravity on Earth, where would we end up? _________________
8. Bigger objects have ______________________ gravity.
9. The Sun has more gravitational pull than the Earth because it is ___________.

Space Perspectives

TARGETING SCIENCE YEAR 6 © PASCAL PRESS ISBN: 9781925726558

Reason for the Season

What do you know about the **seasons**? Would you have as big a seasonal change in Brisbane, compared say, to somewhere like Canada? Can you explain why?

https://clickv.ie/w/_ygx

Use this QR code to access a video on this topic.

Perhaps this experiment will help you to understand the reason for the seasons.

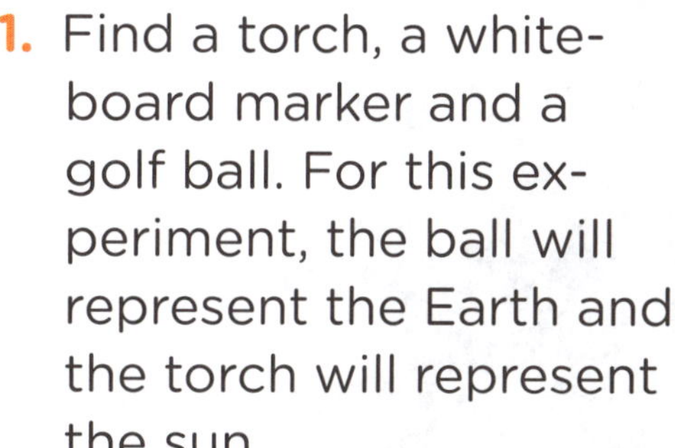

1. Find a torch, a whiteboard marker and a golf ball. For this experiment, the ball will represent the Earth and the torch will represent the sun.

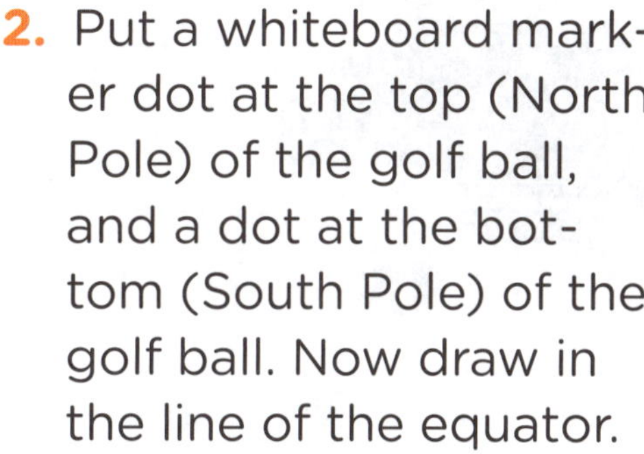

2. Put a whiteboard marker dot at the top (North Pole) of the golf ball, and a dot at the bottom (South Pole) of the golf ball. Now draw in the line of the equator.

AXIAL TILT OF THE EARTH

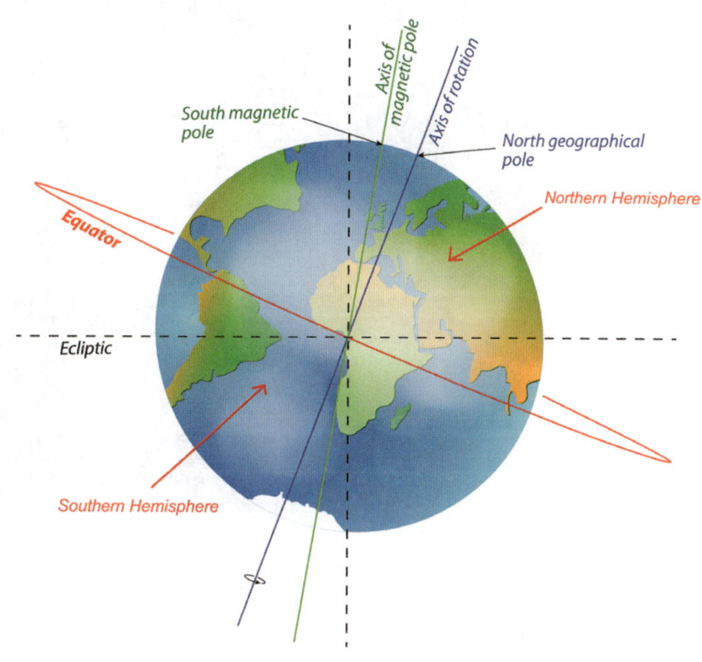

3. Put a cross where Australia would be (you might need to look at a picture of a globe) and a cross where Canada might be.

4. Turn out the lights.

5. Hold the torch in one hand and shine it at the centre of the golf ball.

6. Hold the golf ball up high and in the ray of the torch. Hold the ball straight up and down so that the Equator is running directly around it.

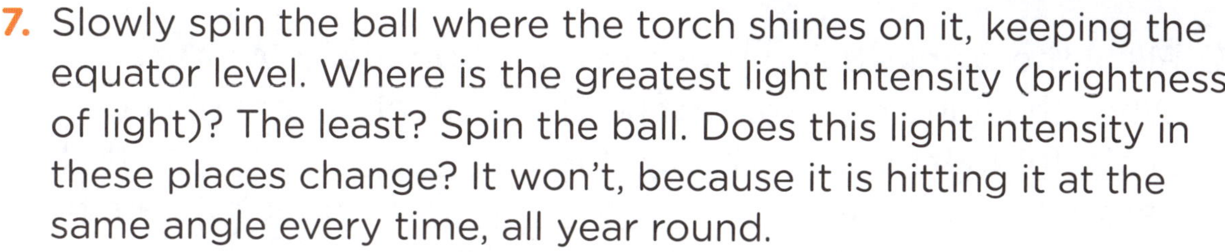

7. Slowly spin the ball where the torch shines on it, keeping the equator level. Where is the greatest light intensity (brightness of light)? The least? Spin the ball. Does this light intensity in these places change? It won't, because it is hitting it at the same angle every time, all year round.

This is not the case in real life, because Earth is not straight up and down from its poles, but on an angle. The axis of the Earth is an imaginary line that runs through the poles and the Earth rotates around it. If you look at the diagram below, you will see the axis, and the angle of the Earth.

Changing Seasons

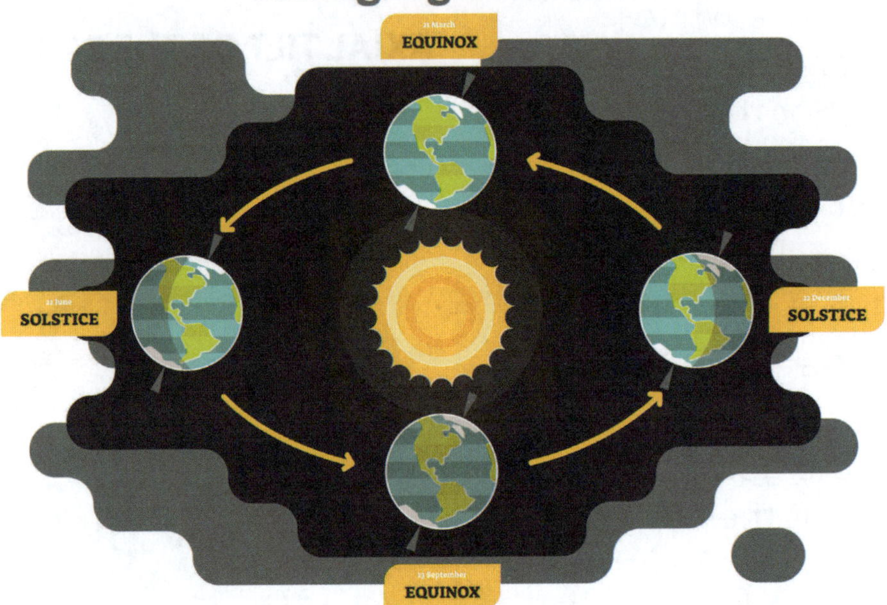

8. Repeat the experiment with the ball on an angle. What are you noticing now, and how it is different for the two continents?

Sometimes the Northern or Southern hemisphere gets more or less light, because the axis of the Earth is tilted. When the Earth revolves around the Sun, sometimes the axis is tilted towards the Sun, and sometimes it is tilted away from the Sun. This is what causes the seasons.

1. On the diagram above, in which position would it be summer-time in the Northern Hemisphere? ________________

2. Why is it summer? Please try to use the words axis and light intensity.

____

3. Fill in the blanks using these words: Summer / Winter
When the Sun's rays are striking the Earth at a more direct angle, for more hours in a day, it is ________________ on that part of the Earth. It is ________________ when the rays are not direct and shine for less hours in the day.

 TARGETING SCIENCE YEAR 6 © PASCAL PRESS ISBN: 9781925726558

Concepts:

Stars are made up of burning hot gases and emit electromagnetic radiation.

The sun looks brighter than other stars because it is closest to Earth.

Have you ever looked up at the night sky and wondered what makes stars shine? Stars are massive, **luminous spheres** of burning hot gases mostly made up of hydrogen and helium. Stars produce energy in the form of **electromagnetic radiation**, which includes radio waves, microwaves, infrared radiation, visible light, ultraviolet radiation, x-rays, and gamma rays.

Define It!

electromagnetic radiation: energy in the form of electric and magnetic waves

luminous: producing light

spectrum: a range of waves

sphere: a round, solid object

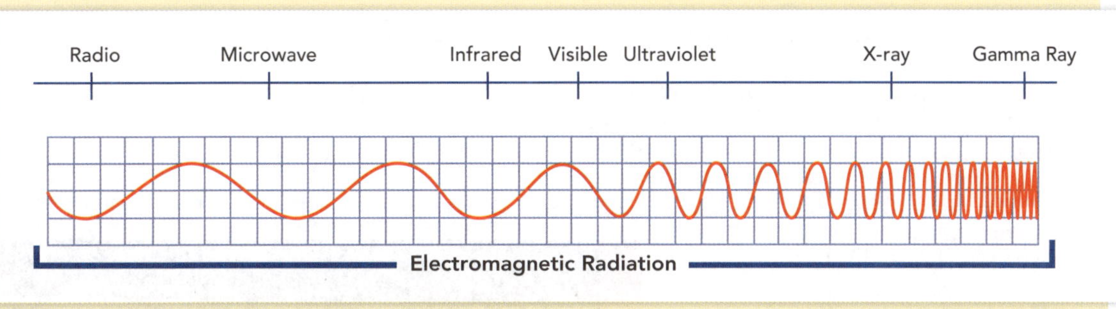

When we see the stars sparkle, we are really seeing the portion of the electromagnetic **spectrum** that is visible light.

Our sun is also a star—the only star in our solar system. Eight large planets and their moons, as well as dwarf planets, asteroids, comets, and meteors, all orbit the sun. The sun appears brighter than any other star in our sky because it is closest to Earth.

Write *true* or *false*.

1. The sun is the only star in our solar system. ________
2. Stars are mostly made up of visible light. ________
3. When we see the stars shine, we are really seeing the x-rays of the electromagnetic spectrum. ________
4. The sun appears brighter than other stars because it is hotter than they are. ________

Size of the Sun

Concept:

The sun is an average size compared to other stars.

The sun is the largest and most massive object in our solar system. It measures 1,392,000 km across and weighs so much that its number of kilograms contains 30 zeros. You could fit 1.3 million Earths inside the sun. Even though the sun is the largest object in our solar system, it is not the largest object in the universe. In **comparison** to the other hundreds of billions of stars in the sky, the sun is an average size. One of the largest known stars, VY Canis Majoris, is so big it's nearly impossible to **fathom** If you put VY Canis Majoris in the centre of our solar system, its outer edges would reach past the orbit of Saturn!

Define It!

comparison: the act of saying how two things are the same or different

disk: a flat, circular object

fathom: to understand the reason for something

reflection: something that shows the effect or existence of something else

The sun looks like it's the largest star in the sky when you are standing on Earth. But this is not a **reflection** of its size. We see the sun as a **disk** instead of a tiny dot because it is much, much closer to Earth than any other star.

The sun is the largest object in our solar system.

Answer the questions.

1. Why do we see the sun as a disk instead of a tiny dot?

____

____

2. How large is the sun compared to other stars? ____________________

3. How large is the sun compared to Earth?

____

TARGETING SCIENCE YEAR 6 © PASCAL PRESS ISBN: 9781925726558

Distance from Earth

Concept: The next-closest star to Earth is light-years away.

Define It!

astronomical unit: the distance from the sun to Earth

light-year: the distance that light travels in one year

The sun is nearly 150 million km from Earth. This distance is measured as an **astronomical unit**. The next-closest star to Earth is named Proxima Centauri, which is 271,000 astronomical units away. However, even though Proxima Centauri is the next-closest star to us, we can't see it without a telescope. This is because it is smaller and less luminous than other stars in the sky.

Since most stars are even farther away than Proxima Centauri, we don't usually measure their distances in astronomical units. Instead, we measure them in **light-years**. Light travels at the speed of 300,000 km per second. That's about seven times around Earth in one second! A light-year is the distance that light can travel in an entire year—about 9.46 trillion km. Proxima Centauri is 4.2 light-years away. The brightest star in our sky, named Sirius, is more than twice the distance from Earth as Proxima Centauri.

Answer the questions.

1. About how many kilometres is 1 astronomical unit? ______________________

2. How many astronomical units away from Earth is Proxima Centauri?

   ____

3. How many light-years away from Earth is Proxima Centauri? ______________________

4. About how many kilometres is 1 light-year? ______________________

Distance from the Sun

Skill:

Interpret information from graphic images.

The *heliosphere* is a large area of space surrounding the sun and our solar system. Solar wind from the sun protects objects inside the heliosphere against the pressures from interstellar space. Think of the heliosphere as a huge magnetic bubble that repels the gases from the rest of our galaxy. The next-closest star to Earth, Proxima Centauri, is located far outside the heliosphere.

Use the diagram to answer the questions.

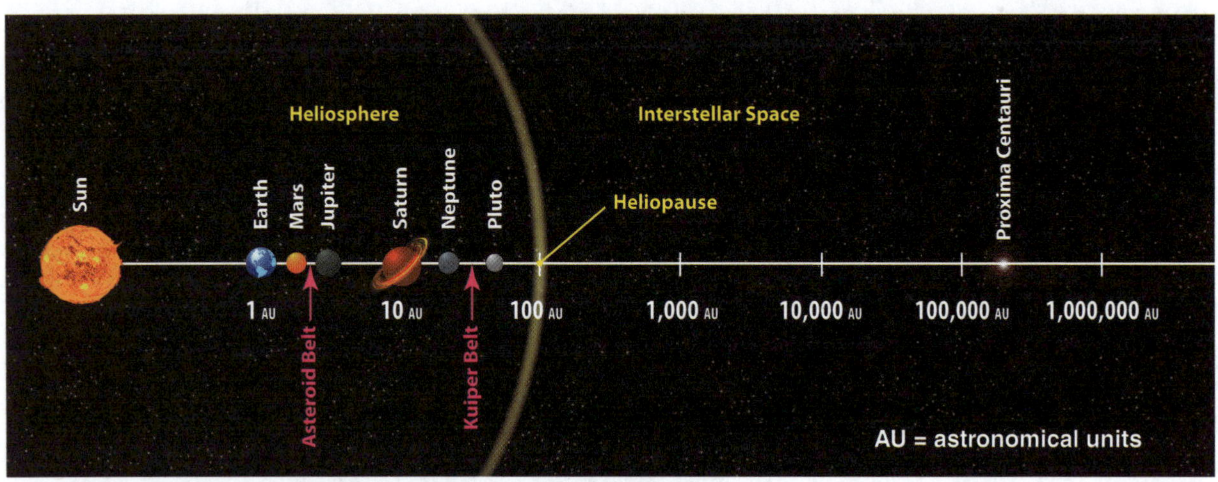

1. The heliosphere ends about how many astronomical units from the sun?

___

2. About how far is Jupiter from the sun?

___

3. Since 1 astronomical unit equals about 150 million km, about how many kilometres is Saturn from the sun?

___

4. Rounding up, Proxima Centauri is 300,000 astronomical units from the sun. Neptune is about 30 astronomical units from the sun. About how many times farther away is Proxima Centauri than Neptune?

___

Space Perspectives

TARGETING SCIENCE YEAR 6 © PASCAL PRESS ISBN: 9781925726558

Toilet Paper Solar System

Skills:

Conduct experiments and analyse results.

When we talk about distances or the amount of space between objects in the universe, we are talking about such large numbers that they are nearly impossible to imagine. It helps to understand how far away objects are in space—even within our own solar system. In this activity, you will use toilet paper to show the relative distance of each of the planets from the sun.

What You Need

- pictures of the 8 planets: Mercury, Venus, Earth, Mars, Jupiter, Saturn, Uranus, Neptune
- marker
- scissors
- roll of toilet paper
- a very long hallway, large room, or outdoor space

Directions

1. Print out pictures of each of the eight planets of the solar system. Label each planet.
2. Choose a point at one end of the hallway as your starting point.
3. Arrange the planets in a straight line across the width of the hallway. The planets should be lined up from closest to farthest from the sun: Mercury, Venus, Earth, Mars, Jupiter, Saturn, Uranus, Neptune.
4. Read the information in the purple column of the chart on page 32 to find each planet's distance from the sun. Then place the appropriate number of toilet paper sheets next to each planet to indicate its distance from the sun. Round up to the nearest toilet paper sheet.

Toilet Paper Solar System

Planet	True distance from sun in kilometres	Distance from sun in toilet paper sheets (30,109,336 kilometres/sheet)	Distance from sun in metres (scale)
Mercury	57,910,007	1.9	0.2
Venus	108,199,995	3.6	0.4
Earth	149,599,951	5.0	0.6
Mars	227,939,920	7.6	0.9
Jupiter	778,330,257	25.9	3
Saturn	1,429,400,028	47.5	5.4
Uranus	2,870,989,228	95.4	11
Neptune	4,504,299,580	150.0	17

What Did You Discover?

1. Count how many sheets there are between Mars and Jupiter. About how many kilometres are there between them?

2. Count how many sheets there are between Mercury and Neptune. About how many kilometres are there between them?

3. Look at the "True distance from sun" column of the chart. How many kilometres are there between Saturn and Uranus?

4. If Proxima Centauri were included in this activity, 1,325,560 sheets of toilet paper would be needed to measure its distance from the sun! If 5 sheets equals 0.58 metres, how many metres away from the starting point would the toilet paper for Proxima Centauri reach?

TARGETING SCIENCE YEAR 6 © PASCAL PRESS ISBN: 9781925726558

Spaceship Travels

Imagine that you could board a spaceship that travels at the speed of light. The spaceship is headed to Proxima Centauri to investigate the next-closest star to Earth. Write about your flight there and what types of things you hope to see when you arrive. Then tell what actually happens once you get to the star! Use information and details from what you've read.

Skill:

Write narratives to develop real or imagined experiences or events.

The Night Sky - a First Nations Perspecitive

https://clickv.ie/w/wtgx

Use this QR code to access a video on this topic.

For thousands of years, First Nations Peoples made observations about the patterns and motions of stars and other elements in the night sky. The beginning of a season, a ceremony time, harvest time, a special meeting or travel could be indicated by a particular star or constellation becoming visible. The phases of the moon and position of the Sun was observed and communicated as a method of timekeeping.

By using rock paintings, songs, petroglyphs (images engraved into rocks) dances, stone arrangements and oral language they have tracked time and followed ancient traditions for millennia (thousands of years). They have learned the language of country by looking to the night sky to forecast and measure time and important patterns.

Here are some examples:

The Ngarrindjeri Peoples – Southern Coorong district SA - used the number of full moons to record the age of children under the age of one.

Peramangk Peoples - Hahndorf area of South Australia – Marked each new moon on a digging stick to record their age.

Ngemba, Kamilaroi and Euahlayi Peoples - north western New South Wales - appearance of Dhinawan (the emu) in the Milky Way indicates to the that it is time to harvest emu eggs.

The Tiwi Peoples describe the planets as wives of the moon, as they follow the same path across the sky, in what astronomers now call a planetary parade.

Yolngu People - north eastern Arnhem Land - use Venus to time the commencement of a special ceremony to celebrate the first rising of Venus, the Morning Star, as it transitions from the Evening Star.

The Pitjantjatjara Peoples - central Australian desert - know that the appearance of the constellation Pleiades in the dawn sky indicates the beginning of the cold season.

Yirrkala Peoples - east Arnhem Land in the Northern Territory - visibility of Scorpius in the morning sky indicates the beginning of the beche de mer (sea cucumber) trading season.

 TARGETING SCIENCE YEAR 6 © PASCAL PRESS ISBN: 9781925726558

Different Types of Stars

The night sky is filled with thousands of stars we can see and billions of stars we cannot see. If you look closely, you will notice that not all stars look alike. Some are larger than others and some are different colours. Stars can be red, yellow, white, or blue. Blue stars are generally the hottest and biggest stars, while red stars are usually the smallest and coolest.

Our sun is **classified** as a yellow **dwarf star**. However, this name is **misleading** for two reasons. The first reason is that the sun is not very small; it is an average size for a star. The second reason is that the sun is not actually yellow. If you were to see our sun from space, you would see that it is pure white. The sun appears yellow to us because Earth's atmosphere changes the colour of the light from the sun.

Define It!

classify: to arrange people or things into groups based on how they are alike

dwarf star: a star of relatively small size and low brightness

misleading: causing to believe something that is not true

Concepts:

Stars are classified by colour, size, and temperature.

Our sun is an average-sized star.

Answer the questions.

1. What are the different colours that stars can be?

____

2. Name two reasons why calling our sun a "yellow dwarf star" is misleading.

____

____

Constellations

Concepts:

Some stars appear grouped together in the sky in formations called constellations.

People have been gazing up at the stars for thousands of years. Long ago, we noticed that certain stars appear to be grouped together and that those groups form pictures called **constellations**. Stars that belong to the same constellation are not always close to one another in space. For example, the stars in the constellation Orion range from 243 light-years to 1,360 light-years away from Earth! Yet all the stars that we can see from Earth (without a powerful telescope) belong to one **galaxy**, our very own Milky Way.

Constellations are usually named after the pictures they form or **mythological figures**. You may already be familiar with some well-known constellations. Have you ever seen the Big Dipper or Orion? The Big Dipper is a series of stars that look like they form the handle and cup of a ladle or a large soup spoon. The stars of Orion look like they form the shape of a hunter holding a bow and arrow.

Define It!

constellation: a group of stars that form a shape in the sky and has been given a name

galaxy: any one of the very large groups of stars that make up the universe

mythological figure: a character based on or described in a myth

Connect the dots to form two constellations. Then label the *Big Dipper* and *Orion*.

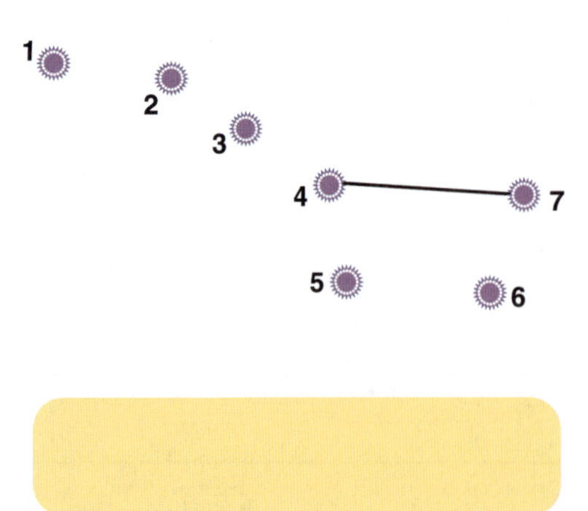

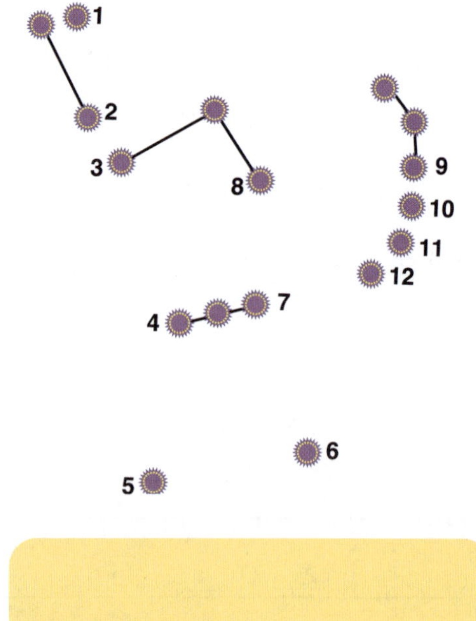

Space Perspectives

TARGETING SCIENCE YEAR 6 © PASCAL PRESS ISBN: 9781925726558

Shifting Skies

Define It!

position: the place where something is in relation to other things

If you watch the night sky throughout the year, you will notice that the stars do not stay in the same place. As the months go by, the familiar constellations slowly shift from view and new constellations take their place. For example, if you live in North America, you can see Orion during the winter and spring months. However, it disappears under the horizon during the summer and autumn months. This is because of Earth's orbit around the sun. As Earth travels through space, our view of the stars changes. Since it takes one year for Earth to orbit the sun, it also takes one year for a constellation to travel out of view and return to its original place.

Because Earth is always rotating, the stars also change **position** in the sky throughout the night—just as the sun changes position during the day. Some constellations rise in the east and set in the west, but others stay in the sky all night.

Summer

Winter

Fill in the correct answer.

1. The stars move across the sky each night because of _____.

   Ⓐ Earth's orbit around the sun

   Ⓑ Earth's rotation

   Ⓒ their movement in the galaxy

   Ⓓ the sun's rising and setting

2. Constellations change as the seasons change because of _____.

   Ⓐ Earth's orbit around the sun

   Ⓑ Earth's rotation

   Ⓒ Earth's tilt on its axis

   Ⓓ Earth's spherical shape

Concepts:

Different constellations are visible during different times of year because of Earth's orbit around the sun.

Seeing Stars

Skill:

Interpret information from graphic images.

Different constellations are visible to us during different seasons. Look at the diagram below. First connect each set of dots to see four constellations. Then use the following information to answer the questions.

- Orion is most visible during the winter in North America.
- Earth orbits the sun in an anticlockwise direction.
- The Southern Hemisphere of Earth experiences opposite seasons from the Northern Hemisphere.

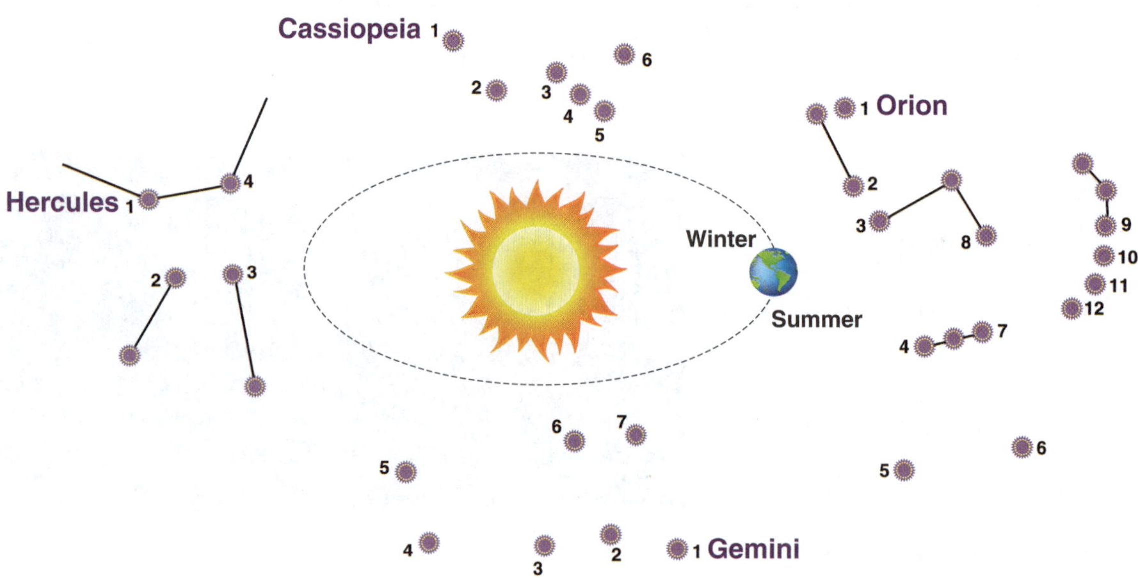

1. During which season is Hercules best visible to North America? ____________

2. During which season is Gemini best visible to North America? ____________

3. During which season is Orion best visible to South America? ____________

Space Perspectives

  ISBN: 9781925726558

Vocabulary Practice

Skill: Apply content vocabulary.

Use the vocabulary words to complete the sentences. Then unscramble the shaded letters to decode the secret message.

position	classify	misleading	dwarf star
galaxy	mythological figures	constellations	

1. Scientists __ __ __ __ __ __ __ __ our sun as a yellow __ __ __ __ __ __ __ __ __.

2. Many __ __ __ __ __ __ __ __ __ __ __ __ __ __ are named after the shapes they form or __ __ __ __ __ __ __ __ __ __ __ __ __ __ __ __ __ __ __.

3. Stars change __ __ __ __ __ __ __ __ in the night sky.

4. Calling our sun a dwarf star is __ __ __ __ __ __ __ __ __ __ because it is actually an average size for a star.

5. All of the stars we can see belong to the same __ __ __ __ __ __.

The constellation __ __ __ __ __ __, Latin for "twins," contains 85 stars that are visible from Earth without a telescope.

Space Perspectives

Shoe Box Planetarium

Skill:

Create models to represent scientific concepts.

In this activity, you will research a constellation and create a miniature planetarium for viewing the stars.

What You Need

- shoe box
- black construction paper
- compass or sharp point
- tracing paper
- scissors
- tape
- 5 cent coin
- ruler

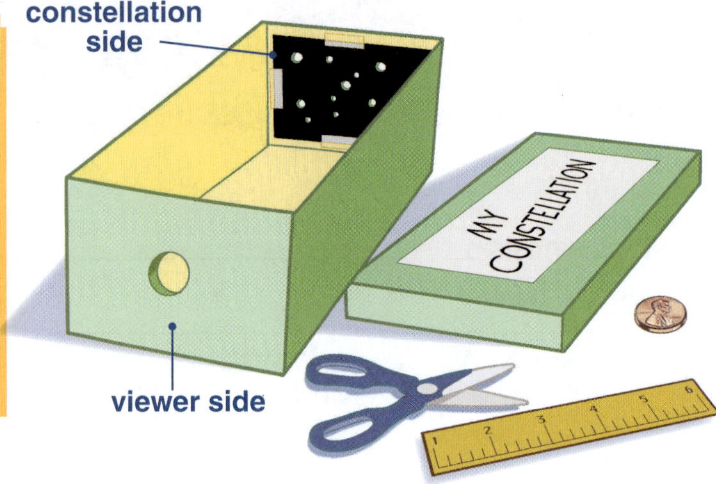

Directions

1. Choose a constellation to research. Complete the form on page 41. Print out a 10 x 15 cm picture of the constellation.
2. Using the ruler, measure the length and width of one end of the shoe box and make a dot in the centre. Place a coin on the dot and trace it. This will be your viewer.
3. Using the scissors, carefully cut out the circle so that the view hole is the size of the traced coin.
4. On the opposite outside end of the shoe box, draw a line where the lid meets the side. Remove the lid.
5. Using the ruler, mark 2 cm from the bottom and 2 cm from each side. Then cut out the rectangle as shown.
6. Cut black construction paper so it will fully cover the rectangular opening.
7. Use tracing paper to copy your constellation, and then place it on top of the black paper. Poke holes through the tracing paper and the black paper where the stars are located. Be sure to make larger holes for brighter stars and smaller holes for dimmer stars.
8. Tape the black paper over the rectangular opening on the inside, with the constellation correctly facing the viewer.
9. Look at your constellation through the viewer!

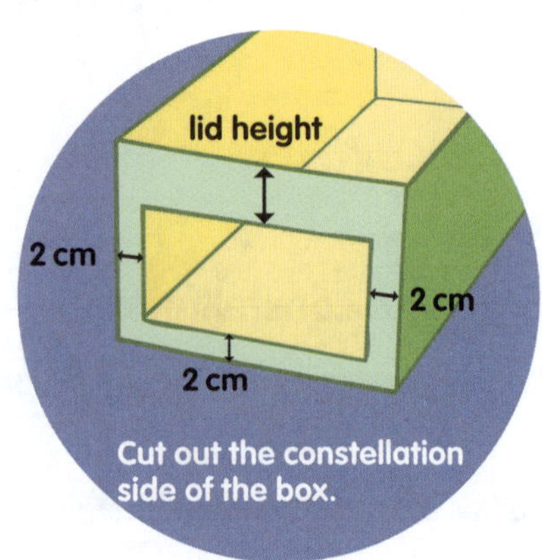

TARGETING SCIENCE YEAR 6 © PASCAL PRESS ISBN: 9781925726558

Your Constellation

Draw a constellation that you would like to see in the night sky. An example is show below.

Answer these questions about your constellation

Name: ____________________

Origin of name: ____________________

____

Number of stars: ____________________

Season best viewed: ____________________

Name three or four constellations that border your constellation.

____

____

Name of brightest star: ____________________

Special features found in your constellation, such as galaxies or meteor showers:

____

____

____

Make a Constellation

Skill:

Present information through graphic images and text.

Space Perspectives

Pretend that the dots on this page are stars. Connect dots to make your own constellation. Then name your constellation and tell what picture the connected dots make.

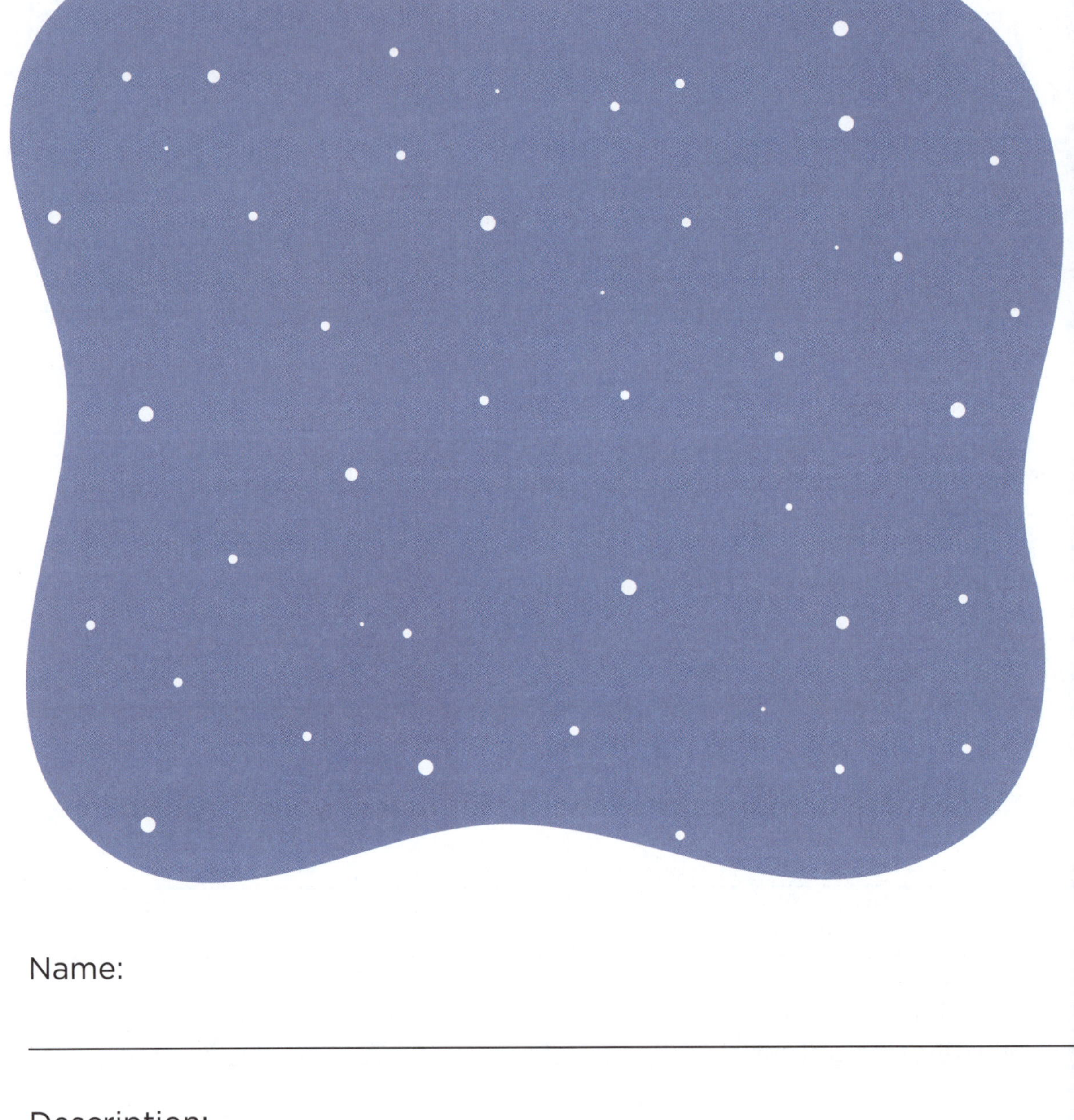

Name:

___

Description:

___

___

___

TARGETING SCIENCE YEAR 6 © PASCAL PRESS ISBN: 9781925726558

Patterns of Daylight

Earth's **climate** varies greatly from region to region and season to season. One reason for this is that patterns of daylight can be very different in different parts of the world. At the North and South Poles, the sun rises and sets only once each year. Six months of daylight are followed by six months of darkness. Because it is dark for such a long time, the poles get very cold. And because the poles are frozen, it is difficult to heat them up once the sun does shine.

The situation is much different at the **equator**. Each day throughout the year has roughly 12 hours of daylight and 12 hours of darkness. As a result, the temperature at the equator is nearly **constant** throughout the year. It is always warm at the equator. With the same amount of light and darkness every day, the areas near the equator do not have a chance to get cold like the poles do.

Define It!

climate: the weather conditions in an area over a long period of time

constant: occurring continuously over a period of time

equator: an imaginary line drawn around Earth equally distant from the North and South Poles

The sun shines throughout the night during summer at the North and South Poles.

Concept:

Earth's climate varies greatly between seasons and regions.

Write *true* or *false*.

1. Earth's temperature is nearly constant at the equator. ____________
2. The sun rises and sets only once a year at the poles. ____________
3. Earth's climate is similar at the poles and the equator. ____________
4. Patterns of daylight impact the temperature in different parts of the world. ____________

Angle of Sunlight

Concept:

The sun shines at different angles because of the curvature of Earth.

Define It!

atmosphere: a thin layer of gases that surrounds Earth

curvature: arching or bending

horizon: the line where the sky and Earth appear to meet

reflect: to cast back from a surface

Because of the **curvature** of Earth, the sun shines at different angles in different places. While the sun shines almost directly overhead at the equator, it remains low on the **horizon** at the poles. Because it is at an angle, the sunlight at the poles travels farther through the **atmosphere** than the sunlight that hits the equator. The atmosphere absorbs and **reflects** some of the sun's energy. So the sunlight that reaches the poles is weaker than the sunlight that reaches the equator.

12 p.m. at the equator

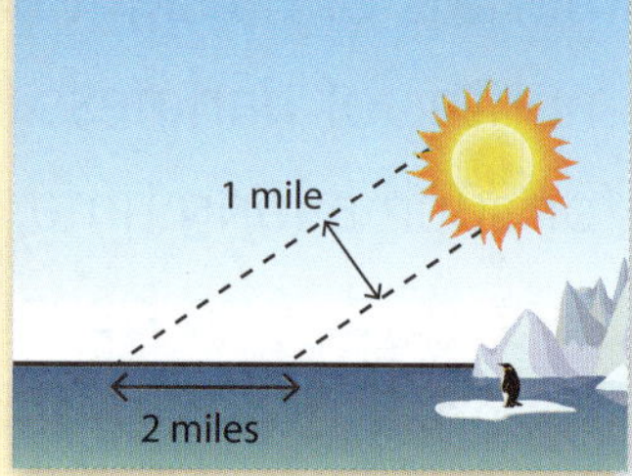

12 p.m. at the poles

A sunbeam that hits the ground at an angle also spreads over a greater area than a sunbeam that comes from overhead. This further reduces the amount of solar energy that the poles receive. With less solar energy, temperatures at the poles remain low.

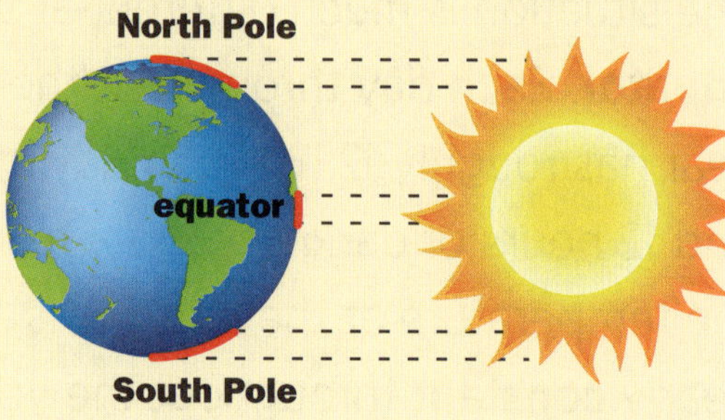

You can estimate the angle of the sun in the sky by the length of your shadow. The longer your shadow is, the greater the angle of the sun. Use this information to answer the questions.

1. If you're standing at the South Pole, will your shadow be longer or shorter than where you live? Why?

____

____

2. Where is your shadow shorter—Far North Queensland or southern Tasmania? Why?

____

____

Climate

TARGETING SCIENCE YEAR 6 © PASCAL PRESS ISBN: 9781925726558

Landscapes and Weather Patterns

Concept: Landscape and weather impact regional climates.

Certain features of Earth's **landscape**, such as soil, water, trees, and even towns and cities, absorb energy. This results in warmer temperatures. But snow does just the opposite. Snow reflects 90% of the sun's energy and sends it back into space. Snow is one more reason the North and South Poles are so cold.

Define It!

landscape: the visible features of a region

Yet another reason the poles are so cold is the weather. Some types of clouds increase the surface temperatures on Earth. They act like a blanket that keeps heat close to the ground. But because the climate is so dry at the poles, there are rarely any clouds in the sky. There are, however, strong winds that blow most of the surface heat away.

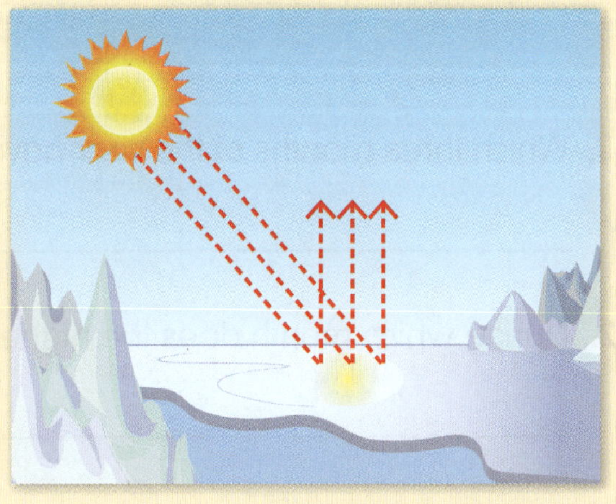

Name one feature of the landscape and two features of the weather at Earth's poles. Explain how each of these features help create cold temperatures.

Landscape: ______________________________

Weather: ______________________________

____

____

Climate

South Pole vs. North Pole

Skill:

Interpret information in graphic representations.

The South Pole is much colder than the North Pole. One reason for this is that the North Pole is located in the middle of an ocean. Regions near the ocean are warmer because the ocean absorbs heat. In comparison, the South Pole is on the continent of Antarctica, around 1300 km from the nearest sea. Another reason is that the South Pole is at a higher elevation, or height above sea level, than the North Pole. Areas of higher elevation have colder temperatures.

Look at this chart of average monthly temperatures at the South Pole and answer the questions.

South Pole													
Month	**Jan**	**Feb**	**Mar**	**Apr**	**May**	**Jun**	**Jul**	**Aug**	**Sep**	**Oct**	**Nov**	**Dec**	**Year**
Average high C°	-25.9	-38.1	-50.3	-54.2	-53.9	-54.4	-55.9	-55.6	-55.1	-48.4	-36.9	-26.5	-46.3
Average low C°	-29.4	-42.7	-57.0	-61.2	-61.7	-61.2	-62.8	-62.5	-62.4	-53.8	-40.4	-29.3	-52.0

1. Which three months of the year have the lowest average temperatures?

____

2. During which month does the highest average temperature occur?

____

3. Winter (January) temperatures at the North Pole can range from about –43°C to –26°C. How does this compare with winter (June) temperatures at the South Pole?

____

____

____

____

Climate

TARGETING SCIENCE YEAR 6 © PASCAL PRESS ISBN: 9781925726558

Skill: Apply content vocabulary.

Select from the vocabulary words to complete the sentences.
Then unscramble the shaded letters to decode the secret message.

constant	horizon	equator	landscape
climate	atmosphere	reflect	curvature

1. Because the ___ ___ ___ ___ ___ ___ ___ is so dry at the poles, there are rarely any clouds in the sky.

2. It is much warmer at the ___ ___ ___ ___ ___ ___ ___ than it is at the North and South Poles.

3. The ___ ___ ___ ___ ___ ___ ___ ___ ___ of Earth impacts the angle at which sunlight hits different parts of the planet.

4. Sunlight travels farther through the ___ ___ ___ ___ ___ ___ ___ ___ ___ ___ to reach the North and South Poles.

5. Certain features of Earth's ___ ___ ___ ___ ___ ___ ___ ___ ___ absorb energy, which creates warmer temperatures.

The North Pole is part of the ___ ___ ___ ___ ___ ___ region, which is a word that also means "very cold."

Climate

Too Cold to Snow

Skills:

Make observations, create charts, and analyse data.

When you think of the North and South Poles, you likely imagine that snow falls throughout the year. However, the poles receive a surprisingly small amount of snowfall, and their frigid temperatures are partly to blame!

Research the weather conditions and temperatures during a winter month at the North Pole, at the South Pole, and in Buffalo, NY, USA (a city known for high levels of snowfall). Compare your data to see the relationship between temperatures and snowfall.

Materials

- Internet access or an archive of old newspapers
- 3 charts

Directions

1. Create a four-column chart for each location. Write column titles for date, high temperature, low temperature, and precipitation. (See example chart on page 49.)
2. Select a winter month for the three locations. You may want to choose the same month for the two locations in the Northern Hemisphere. (The South Pole's winter months are opposite from the North Pole and Buffalo, NY.)
3. Using the Internet or archived newspaper reports, check the weather and temperature for every day of the month. Archived newspaper reports can be found in many school or community libraries. Monthly weather reports for various locations can also be found using the National Oceanic and Atmospheric Administration (NOAA) website.
4. Record both the high and low temperatures for each day of the month in each location, as well as the amount of precipitation, if any.

Climate

Example Chart

Location:			
Date	**High Temp**	**Low Temp**	**Precipitation**
Feb 1			
Feb 2			
Feb 3			
Feb 4			
Feb 5			
Feb 6			
Feb 7			
Feb 8			
Feb 9			
Feb 10			
Feb 11			
Feb 12			
Feb 13			
Feb 14			

Date	High Temp	Low Temp	Precipitation
Feb 15			
Feb 16			
Feb 17			
Feb 18			
Feb 19			
Feb 20			
Feb 21			
Feb 22			
Feb 23			
Feb 24			
Feb 25			
Feb 26			
Feb 27			
Feb 28			

What Did You Discover?

1. Was there any precipitation at the North and South Poles during the winter month you selected? If so, how much? How did it compare to the snowfall in Buffalo, NY?

____

____

2. At all three locations, on average, was it warmer or colder during periods of precipitation than during dry periods?

____

____

3. What were the lowest temperatures recorded for the month in all three areas? Was there precipitation during this time?

____

____

Regional Climates in Australia

Skill:

Interpret information in graphic representations.

The map below shows the various climate zones of Australia, ranging from the sweltering tropical to cool temperate. Use the map and climate descriptions to answer the questions.

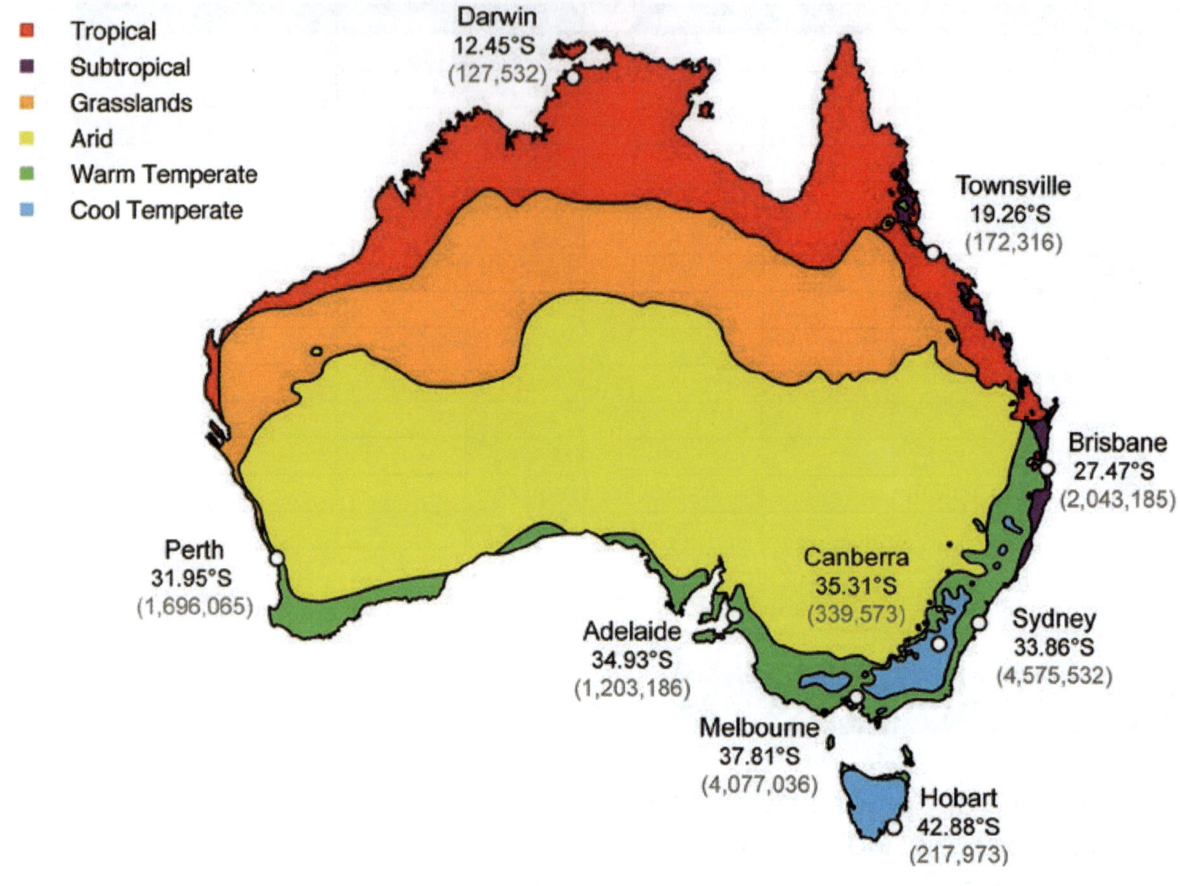

1. How many different types of climate zones are shown on the map? ______

2. Which two climate zones are the direct opposites—one is always warm and one is always cold?

____

3. Which two climate zones cover the smallest areas?

____

4. Which climate zone is the largest in the country?

____

5. Which climate zone do you live in?

____

TARGETING SCIENCE YEAR 6 © PASCAL PRESS ISBN: 9781925726558

Earth's Atmosphere

Define It!

atmosphere: a thin layer of gases that surrounds Earth

environment: the natural world

thrive: to live well; to be healthy and happy

Concepts:

The atmosphere is a layer of gases that surrounds the planet.

The atmosphere traps heat from the sun.

The **atmosphere** is an important part of Earth's **environment**. Because of our atmosphere, living things can survive. The atmosphere is a thin layer of gases that surrounds the planet. It is made up of a mixture of nitrogen, oxygen, carbon dioxide, water vapour, and other gases.

The atmosphere contains the gases that living things need to breathe. It also includes gases that help trap the sun's heat. This keeps temperatures on Earth even. It also allows for water to exist as a liquid. While the atmosphere allows the sun's heat in, it also keeps out harmful rays from the sun. The sun, the atmosphere, and Earth work together so that living things are able to grow and **thrive** on this planet.

Answer the questions.

1. Name three ways the atmosphere makes Earth suitable for living things.

____

____

____

2. How do the atmosphere and the sun work together?

____

____

____

Greenhouse Gases

Concepts:

Greenhouse gases in our atmosphere absorb heat.

The amount of greenhouse gases in our atmosphere is increasing.

Have you ever been in a greenhouse and noticed how warm it is? Greenhouses are designed to keep heat inside, just like our atmosphere. Special gases in our atmosphere called **greenhouse gases** absorb heat. These gases include carbon dioxide, methane, and nitrous oxide.

While greenhouse gases are important for keeping the temperature warm on Earth, these gases can be harmful when higher amounts of them are trapped in our atmosphere. There's a risk that Earth could get too warm. Higher temperatures on Earth could result in global changes, such as droughts, melting ice caps, higher sea levels, and stronger storms. Unfortunately, the amount of greenhouse gases in our atmosphere has been increasing. Human activities are largely responsible for that increase. These activities include mining, transporting, and burning **fossil fuels** such as coal and natural gas, as well as cutting down and burning trees.

Define It!

fossil fuels: fuels such as oil, coal, and natural gas that are formed from the remains of living things

greenhouse gases: gases in the atmosphere that absorb heat from the sun

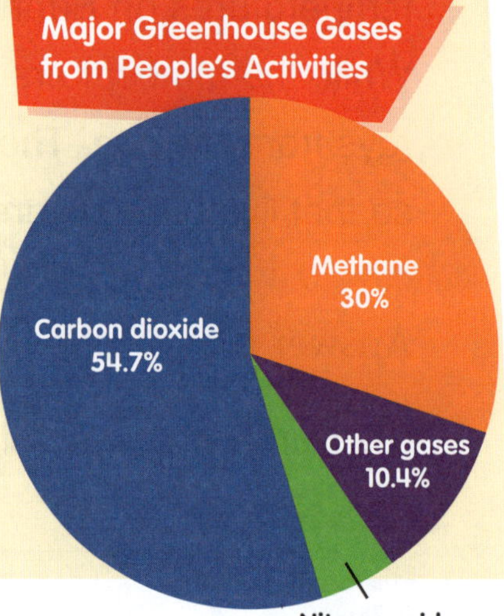

Write *true* or *false*.

1. The greenhouse gas that people create the most of is carbon dioxide. ________

2. All greenhouse gases are harmful. ________

3. The amount of greenhouse gases in our atmosphere has been decreasing. ________

4. Cutting down and burning trees creates greenhouse gases. ________

TARGETING SCIENCE YEAR 6 © PASCAL PRESS ISBN: 9781925726558

Impacts of Cattle Farming

Define It!

emit: to give off or release

livestock: animals that are raised for milk, meat, or other goods

One of the human activities that creates a large amount of harmful greenhouse gas is cattle farming. Two-thirds of the farmland on Earth is used for raising cows, and the demand for **livestock** is expected to rise. The problem is that cows **emit** methane gas through burping, or belching.

Some scientists say that the amount of methane one cow produces in one day is equal to the amount of pollution one car emits in one day. The Food and Agriculture Organization of the United Nations says it is urgent for us to take action right away because large amounts of methane gas are harmful to Earth's atmosphere.

One solution may be to have people reduce the amount of beef we eat. As an alternative, we could follow the example of other countries by adding insects to our diet. The thought of eating bugs might seem unpleasant, but there are many good reasons to use them as a food source. Insects produce a lot less gas than larger animals—about 100 times less. It takes up to 1,000 times less water to raise insects as it does to raise livestock. And eating insects would also help make sure we don't run out of other food sources, such as fish and wild game.

Answer the questions.

1. Cattle farming produces a large amount of which greenhouse gas? ____________

2. How do cows emit greenhouse gas?

____

3. In what ways does eating insects instead of beef help the environment?

____

____

____

Concepts:

Cattle farming creates a large amount of greenhouse gases.

Changes to our diet could help decrease the amount of greenhouse gases released into the atmosphere.

A Closer Look at Greenhouse Gases

Skill:

Interpret information in graphic representations.

This chart shows different sources of greenhouse gas emissions in the United States. Study the chart and answer the questions.

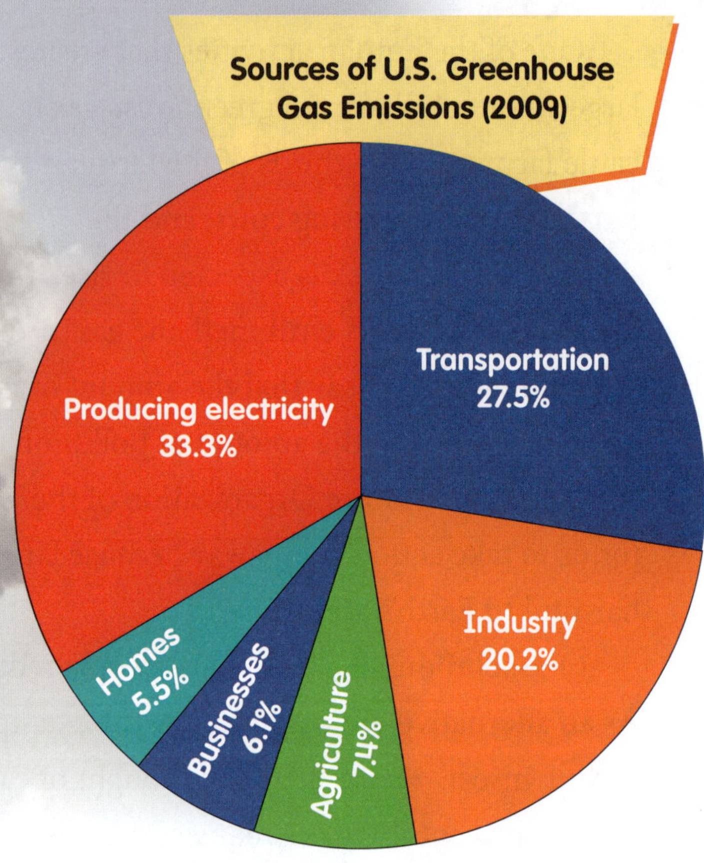

1. What is the highest source of greenhouse gas emissions in the United States? ______________________

2. Homes and businesses account for what percentage of U.S. greenhouse gas emissions? ________%

3. Transportation is the second-highest source of greenhouse gas emissions in the United States. What are some ways people could reduce greenhouse gas emissions from transportation?

____

____

____

____

____

Climate

TARGETING SCIENCE YEAR 6 © PASCAL PRESS ISBN: 9781925726558

Vocabulary Practice

Use the vocabulary words to complete the sentences. Then unscramble the shaded letters to decode the secret message.

atmosphere	environment	thrive	livestock
fossil fuels	greenhouse gases	emit	

1. Life is able to grow and ___ ___ ___ ___ ___ ___ on Earth.

2. Too many ___ ___ ___ ___ ___ ___ ___ ___ ___ ___ ___   ___ ___ ___ ___ ___ can make the planet too warm.

3. The burning of ___ ___ ___ ___ ___ ___   ___ ___ ___ ___ ___ is one human activity that adds harmful gases to our ___ ___ ___ ___ ___ ___ ___ ___ ___ ___.

4. Another activity that increases greenhouse gases is the raising of ___ ___ ___ ___ ___ ___ ___ ___ ___.

5. Cows ___ ___ ___ ___ large amounts of methane gas daily.

6. Eating bugs instead of cows can help save our ___ ___ ___ ___ ___ ___ ___ ___ ___ ___ ___.

The process by which gases hold heat in the air is called the

___ ___ ___ ___ ___ ___ ___ ___ ___ ___   ___ ___ ___ ___ ___ ___.

Skill:

Apply content vocabulary.

Climate

Greenhouse Effect

Skills:

Conduct experiments, record data, and analyse results.

Humans are adding many greenhouse gases to the atmosphere, and carbon dioxide (CO_2) leads the pack. In this experiment, you will observe the impact of increased CO_2 on the temperature of the atmosphere.

What You Need

- 2 aquariums or any other large glass containers
- 3 thermometers
- 2 pieces of thick cardboard
- baking soda
- vinegar
- 2 1-litre bottles and 1 cap
- balloons
- duct tape

Aquarium **A**
(Control)

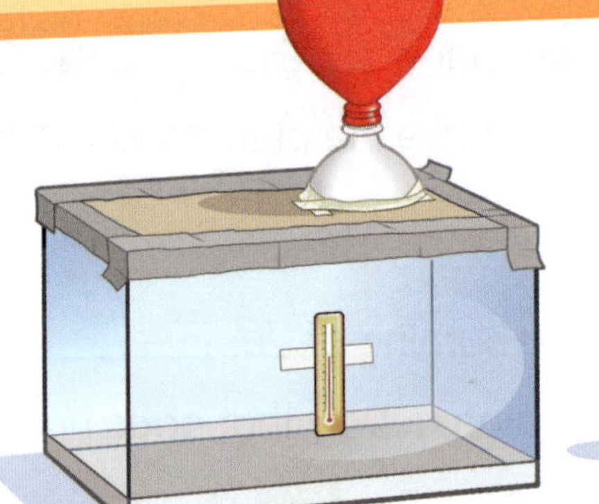

Aquarium **B**
(CO_2)

Directions

1. Tape a thermometer to the inside of each aquarium. Place the aquariums next to windows that get equal amounts of sunlight.
2. Tape one piece of cardboard over the top of Aquarium A.
3. Take one 1-litre bottle. (Keep the bottle cap for Step 8.) Cut off the nozzle. Then cut a hole in the second piece of cardboard to fit the nozzle. Secure the nozzle to the cardboard with duct tape. Then tape the cardboard over the top of Aquarium B as shown.
4. Add 4 tablespoons (80 mL) of vinegar to the uncut litre bottle.
5. Pour 1 teaspoon (5 mL) of baking soda inside a balloon.
6. Stretch the mouth of the balloon over the top of the bottle and hold the balloon upright so that the baking soda pours into the vinegar.
7. The balloon will fill with CO_2 quickly. Remove the balloon from the bottle and seal it by holding the mouth tightly.
8. Attach the balloon to the nozzle on Aquarium B and expel the CO_2 by squeezing the balloon. Quickly screw the cap back onto the nozzle to keep the CO_2 inside.
9. On page 57, record the temperature inside both aquariums, as well as the room temperature.
10. Repeat Steps 4–9 each afternoon for two weeks.

 ISBN: 9781925726558

Day	Time	Aquarium A (Control)	Aquarium B (CO_2)	Room Temperature
Day 1				
Day 2				
Day 3				
Day 4				
Day 5				
Day 6				
Day 7				
Day 8				
Day 9				
Day 10				
Day 11				
Day 12				
Day 13				
Day 14				

What Did You Discover?

1. What did you notice about the temperature of Aquarium A? How did it compare to room temperature?

____

____

2. What did you notice about the temperature of Aquarium B? How did it compare to Aquarium A? How did it compare to room temperature?

____

____

3. What do you think this experiment says about increased levels of CO_2 in our atmosphere?

____

____

TARGETING SCIENCE YEAR 6 © PASCAL PRESS ISBN: 9781925726558

What Is Climate Change?

Concept:

Climate change results in changes to Earth that could make it uninhabitable.

Define It!

climate change: a long-term change in Earth's climate

extinction: the dying out of a species

uninhabitable: unsuitable for living in

Conditions on our planet are constantly changing. Our weather changes daily. Our seasons change four times a year. And our climate can also change. In fact, most scientists agree that we are currently experiencing global **climate change**. Climate change can lead to shifts in temperatures, sea levels, and ocean currents. Together, these factors can change the environment so much that Earth could become **uninhabitable** for many plants and animals. In fact, climate change is one of the most common causes of **extinction** for all species on Earth.

Climate change can be caused by slow, continuous processes such as changes in Earth's orbit or variations in solar activity. These processes happen over very long periods of time. Climate change can also be caused by natural disasters, such as volcanic eruptions and asteroid impacts, which throw dust and debris into the air and block out the sun. For example, the extinction of the dinosaurs was likely caused by global climate change due to an asteroid hitting Earth.

Answer the questions.

1. Which two natural disasters can lead to climate change?

____

2. Which climate change factors can alter the environment to the point it becomes uninhabitable?

____

____

Ice Ages and Global Warming

Concepts:

Earth goes through periods of ice ages and global warming.

Humans are causing the climate to change.

Define It!

glacier: a slowly moving mass of ice

global warming: a gradual increase in the overall temperature of Earth's atmosphere

ice age: a cold period marked by the presence of large ice sheets

Global climate change is nothing new for our planet. There have been at least five major **ice ages**. The most recent began about 2.5 million years ago and lasted until 10,000 years ago. During an ice age, Earth enters periods of global cooling that result in ice and **glaciers** covering large parts of the planet. For example, in the last ice age, much of the Northern Hemisphere was covered in glaciers, and temperatures were, on average, about 5°C cooler than they are today.

For every ice age, there follows a period of **global warming**. Most scientists agree we are currently in the middle of a global warming trend, which is changing the climate for the entire planet. This time, however, the global warming is not the result of slow processes or natural disasters. Humans are causing the climate to change.

Glaciers covered much of the Northern Hemisphere during the last ice age.

Write *true* or *false*.

1. We are currently in a period of global warming. __________

2. Temperatures in the last ice age were, on average, 5°C cooler than they are now. __________

3. The most recent ice age ended 2.5 million years ago. __________

Impact of Humans

Concept:

Too many greenhouse gases trap too much heat in our atmosphere, which can have dire consequences for the climate and habitat.

Define It!

consequence: a result or effect of an action or condition

emit: to give off or release

fossil fuel: a fuel such as coal or gas formed from the remains of living things

greenhouse gas: gases in the atmosphere that absorb heat from the sun

habitat: the natural home or environment of an organism

Earth is warming up more quickly than we've ever seen in modern history. This is because people have been adding heat-trapping gases called **greenhouse gases** to the atmosphere. We've done this by burning **fossil fuels** such as oil, coal, and natural gas. In addition, we've pumped extra greenhouse gases into the atmosphere by raising livestock, which **emit** methane gas as a waste product. Rising global temperatures can have major **consequences** for the climate, resulting in melting ice caps, rising sea levels, stronger storms, and droughts. Even the slightest change in the global average temperature can have an impact. A 0.9°C increase in the average temperature since the year 1880 has led to an 11.5% decrease in the polar ice caps each decade. In addition, the global average sea level has increased 10–20 cm in the last century. All of these changes can lead to **habitat** destruction for many species. In fact, polar bears are being threatened with extinction because their habitat is shrinking so dramatically in such a short time because of climate change.

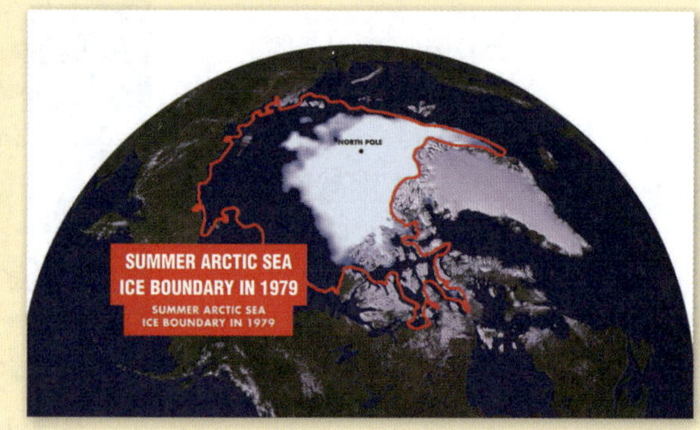

Scientific Visualization Studio, NSIDC, NASA Goddard Space Flight Centre

Complete the sentences.

1. People have been adding ____________________ gases to the atmosphere by burning ____________________ fuels.

2. Melting ice caps, rising sea levels, stronger storms, and ____________________ are the result of rising global ____________________.

Climate

Greenhouse Gas Emissions

Skill: Interpret information from a graph or chart.

This chart shows how greenhouse gas emissions around the world have changed over a 15-year period from 1990 to 2005. Use the chart to answer the questions below.

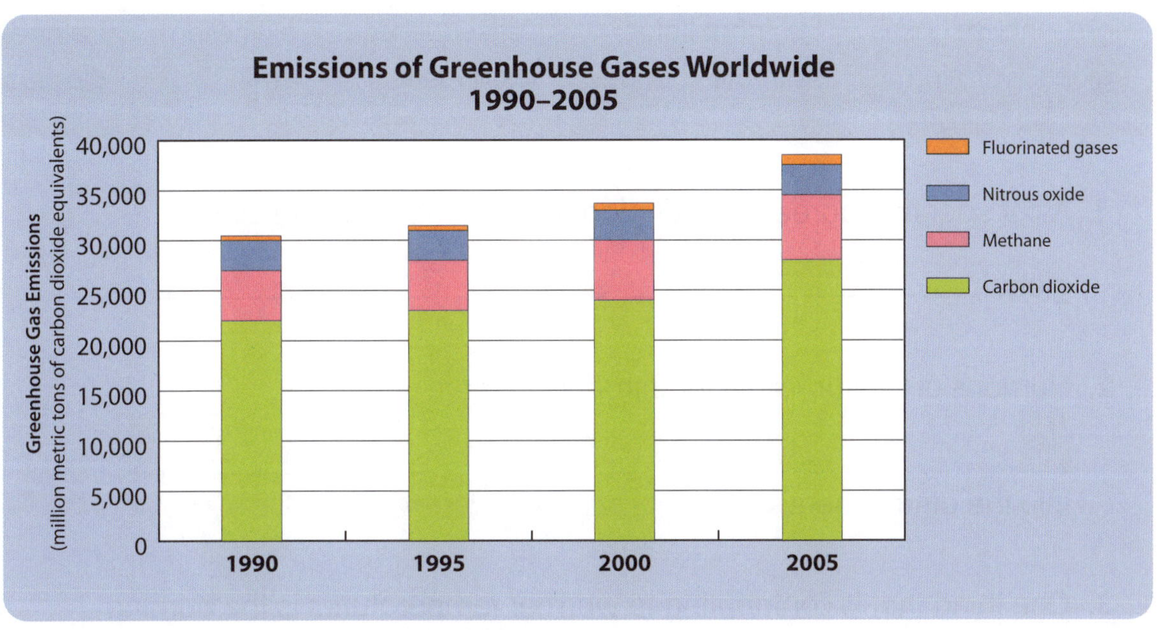

1. Are greenhouse gas emissions increasing, decreasing, or staying the same?

____

2. If 1,000 million equals 1 billion, then about how many metric tons of greenhouse gas emissions were there in 2005? About how many metric tons were there in 1990?

____

____

3. Which greenhouse gas was emitted the most?

____

4. About how much methane gas was emitted in the year 2000?

____

Climate

Vocabulary Pratice

Skill:

Apply content vocabulary.

Select from the vocabulary words to complete the sentences.
Then unscramble the shaded letters to decode the secret message.

greenhouse gases	uninhabitable	consequence	extinction	ice age
global warming	climate change	fossil fuels	emit	glaciers

1. Most scientists agree that our planet is currently experiencing global ___ ___ ___ ___ ___ ___ ___   ___ ___ ___ ___ ___ ___.

2. Humans are responsible for introducing more ___ ___ ___ ___ ___ ___ ___ ___ ___ ___   ___ ___ ___ ___ ___ into the atmosphere.

3. One thing that is contributing to warmer temperatures is the burning of ___ ___ ___ ___ ___ ___   ___ ___ ___ ___ ___.

4. During the last ice age, much of the Northern Hemisphere was covered in ___ ___ ___ ___ ___ ___ ___ ___.

5. Changes in climate can make an environment ___ ___ ___ ___ ___ ___ ___ ___ ___ ___ ___ ___ ___ for many species.

6. Climate change can sometimes lead to the ___ ___ ___ ___ ___ ___ ___ ___ ___ ___ of a species.

The process by which gases hold heat in the atmosphere is called the ___ ___ ___ ___ ___ ___ ___ ___ ___ ___   ___ ___ ___ ___ ___ ___.

Climate

TARGETING SCIENCE YEAR 6 © PASCAL PRESS ISBN: 9781925726558

Melting Ice

The ice cap of the North Pole is a large frozen mass of ice over the Arctic Ocean. The ice sheets of the South Pole are on top of the continent of Antarctica. In this experiment, you will prepare two models—one to represent the North Pole ice cap and another to represent the ice sheets of the South Pole—and you will compare how melting ice impacts both areas.

Skills:

Conduct experiments and draw conclusions about results.

North Pole Model Directions

1. Label one container "North Pole" with the permanent marker.
2. Fill the North Pole container about one-half to two-thirds full with cold tap water. The water represents the Arctic Ocean.
3. Add two ice cubes to the container. The ice cubes represent the polar ice cap.
4. After you add the ice cubes, mark the water level on the side of the container with the marker.

Materials

- Play-Doh® or other modeling clay
- 2 clear plastic containers, about 2 ¼ cups (530 mL) each
- ice cubes (at least 4)
- permanent marker
- measuring cups
- butter knife
- ruler

South Pole Model Directions

1. Label the second container "South Pole" with the marker.
2. Pack clay into the measuring cup until it measures one cup (240 mL).
3. Remove the clay from the measuring cup, using the butter knife to scrape the sides. Place the clay in the South Pole container. There should be space between the clay and the wall of the container all around, and the clay should be fairly flat on top. The clay represents the continent of Antarctica.
4. Add ¼ cup (60 mL) of water to the container. The water should cover only about two-thirds of the clay.
5. Place two ice cubes on top of the clay and press them down lightly. The ice cubes represent the South Pole ice sheets.
6. After you add the ice cubes, mark the water level on the side of the container with the marker.

Melting Ice

Compare the Models

1. Wait for the ice of both models to melt. Do not disturb either of the models during this time.
2. Once the ice has completely melted, look to see if the water level has risen in either of the containers. If the water level has risen, mark the new level with the marker. Measure the amount of rise with the ruler.

What Did You Discover?

1. Did you see the water level rise in the North Pole model? If so, how much?

   ____

2. Did you see the water level rise in the South Pole model? If so, how much?

   ____

3. Based on your results, which pole is of more concern for rising sea levels because of global warming?

   ____

 TARGETING SCIENCE YEAR 6 © PASCAL PRESS ISBN: 9781925726558

Climate Connections

Skill:

Interpret information in graphic representations.

Changes in our atmosphere can have wide-ranging effects on our climate. For example, an increase in greenhouse gas emissions has led to a rise in global temperatures. This chart shows how this one change impacts many aspects of our climate.

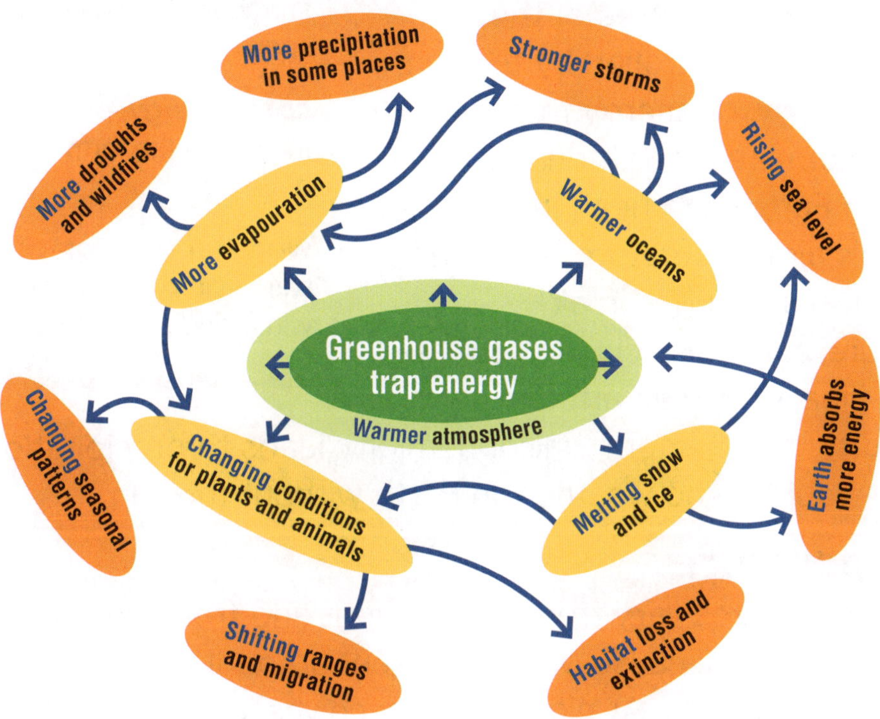

1. A warmer atmosphere due to increases in greenhouse gases leads to warmer oceans. What does having warmer oceans lead to?

___

___

2. What are three factors that lead to changing conditions for plants and animals?

___

___

3. Which factor leads to both increases in precipitation and more droughts?

___

Climate

Concept:

Weather is controlled by the sun.

Define It!

humidity: the amount of moisture in the air

precipitation: water droplets that fall to Earth's surface in the form of rain, snow, sleet, or hail

solar energy: power from the sun in the form of light and heat

weather: the state of the air with regard to temperature, wind, and precipitation

There are three elements that make up the **weather**. They are temperature, wind, and **precipitation**. All three of these elements are controlled by the sun. **Solar energy**, or energy from the sun, determines the amount of heat on Earth. And heat, in turn, controls air temperature. The sun also causes changes in air pressure, and these changes create wind. Finally, the sun affects **humidity**. A higher amount of humidity leads to precipitation. There would be no weather on Earth without the sun.

Temperature

Air temperatures vary from day to night and from season to season. This is because of the different amounts of solar energy that Earth receives. At night, Earth receives less solar energy than during the day. Earth also receives less solar energy during the winter than during the summer. With decreased solar energy, there is less heat. With increased solar energy, there is more heat. These increases and decreases in solar energy determine whether temperatures will be lower or higher.

Write each word in its correct place on the flowchart to show how the sun causes all weather.

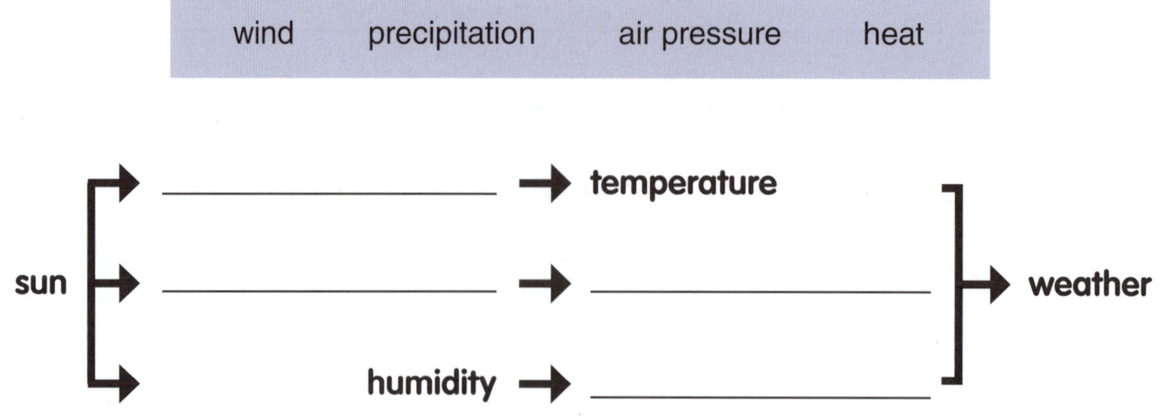

TARGETING SCIENCE YEAR 6 © PASCAL PRESS ISBN: 9781925726558

Define It!

contract: to decrease in size; to shrink

convection current: the circular flow of a substance due to pressure and temperature differences

expand: to increase in size; to enlarge

radiate: to emit energy in the form of rays or waves

regulate: to control or maintain something

Just as the sun **regulates** temperature, it also regulates the wind. Wind is created when Earth's surface absorbs, or takes in, solar energy. Solar energy in the form of heat **radiates** from the surface. This heat warms the air close to the ground. The heated air molecules move faster, causing the air to **expand**. The air also becomes lighter. The weight of all the air above it puts a lot of pressure on the air close to the ground. But when the warm air expands, it decreases the pressure. This causes the warm air to rise.

As the air rises, it cools and **contracts**. Cold air is heavier and applies more pressure; therefore, it tends to sink. Once near the ground, the cold air again becomes warm and rises again. This continuous cycle is called a **convection current**. The convection current, or movement of air from areas of high pressure to areas of low pressure, is what we feel as wind.

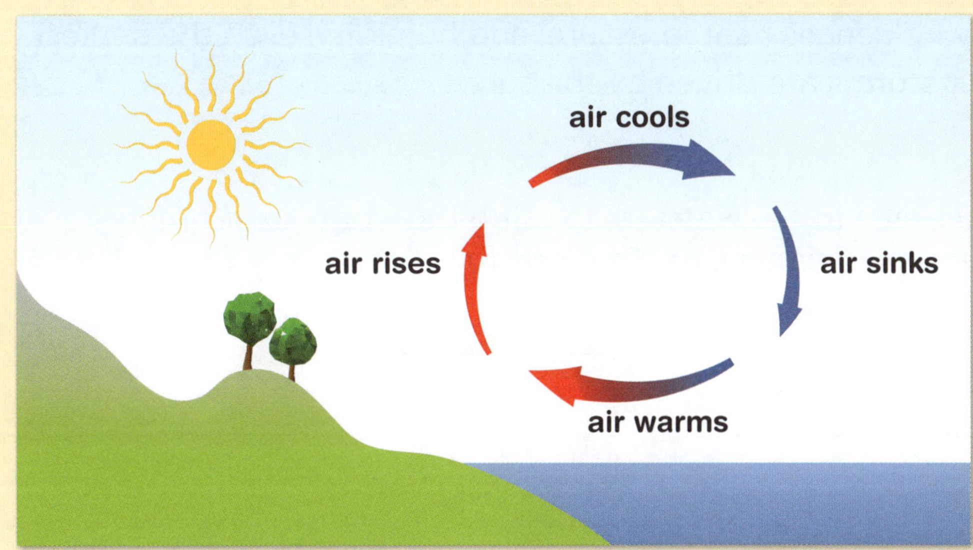

Summarise why warm air rises and cool air sinks.

____

____

____

Concepts:

Wind is created when Earth absorbs solar energy.

Convection currents are what we feel as wind.

TARGETING SCIENCE YEAR 6 © PASCAL PRESS ISBN: 9781925726558

Precipitation

Concept:

The sun powers the water cycle.

Define It!

condense: to convert a gas into a liquid

evaporate: to convert a liquid into a gas

water cycle: the continuous movement of water on Earth

In addition to temperature and wind, the sun also affects precipitation. As solar energy heats Earth's oceans, rivers, and lakes, it causes some of the water to **evaporate** into water vapour. The water vapour rises into the atmosphere, where it begins to cool. As it cools, the water **condenses** into water droplets. The droplets collect in clouds, which get heavier and heavier until they can't hold any more water. Finally, the water is released, and it falls to Earth as precipitation. This cycle of evaporation, condensation, and precipitation is called the **water cycle**.

Dramatic Weather Events

Certain combinations of temperature, wind, and precipitation can sometimes result in dramatic weather events, such as cyclones. These storm systems usually happen when two air masses of different levels of heat, pressure, and humidity meet. Because solar energy influences heat, pressure, and humidity, even the darkest, fiercest storms are driven by the sun.

Label each step in the water cycle using the words *condensation*, *evaporation*, *precipitation*, and *solar energy*.

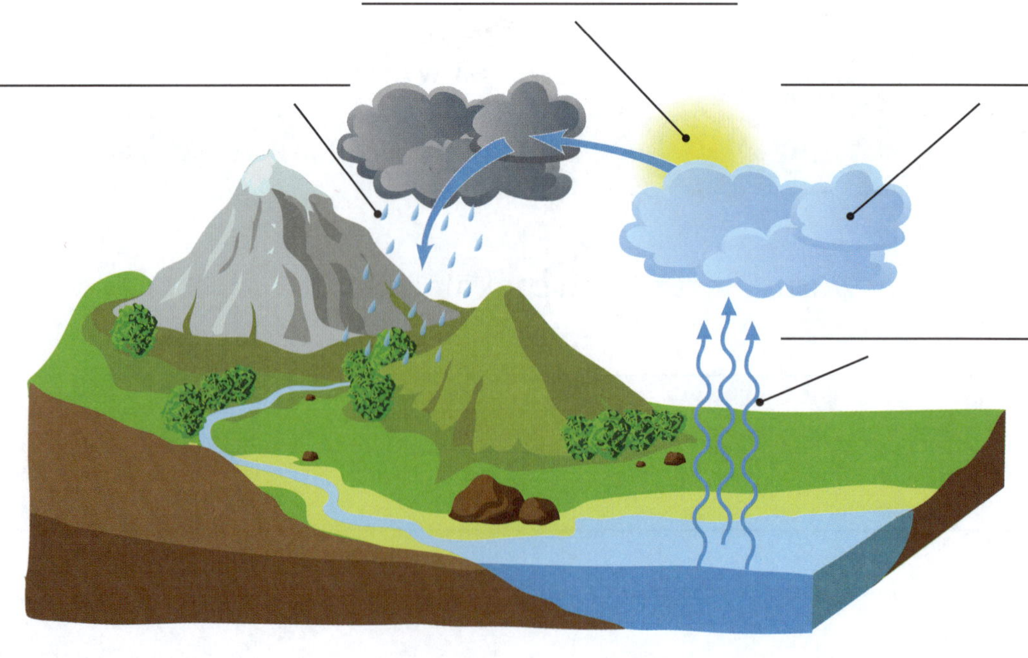

TARGETING SCIENCE YEAR 6 © PASCAL PRESS ISBN: 9781925726558

Skills:

Interpret and identify information in graphic representations.

Look at the diagram of convection currents near the ocean.
Label where the air *warms*, *rises*, *cools*, and *sinks*.
Then label the *solar energy*.

On a sunny day at the beach, the land heats up faster than the ocean. The warmer air over the land rises, so the cooler air over the ocean rushes in to take its place. This creates a wind called a sea breeze. After sunset, the land cools faster than the water, so the air over the ocean is warmer. Describe what you think happens to the movement of air and the direction of the wind.

____

____

____

____

TARGETING SCIENCE YEAR 6 © PASCAL PRESS ISBN: 9781925726558

Egg in a Bottle

Skills:

Conduct experiments and draw conclusions about the results.

In this experiment, you will see the effects of changing air pressure. Air pressure can push an egg into a bottle, and it can also get the egg back out! Because of the use of matches, adult supervision is necessary.

Materials

- hard-boiled egg
- glass bottle or vase with a long, narrow neck (as long as the bottle neck is narrower than the egg)
- matches

Directions

1. Peel the hard-boiled egg, removing all of its shell.
2. Light a match and drop it into the bottle. Repeat this three to four times.
3. Very quickly after the last match goes out, place the egg over the mouth of the bottle. Watch the egg get sucked into the bottle!
4. Tip the bottle upside down and notice that the egg does not come out.
5. To get the egg back out of the bottle, hold the bottle close to your mouth, tilt it, and blow air into it. Be sure to get out of the way, because the egg could come shooting out!

 TARGETING SCIENCE YEAR 6 © PASCAL PRESS ISBN: 9781925726558

What Did You Discover?

1. What do you think the lit matches did to the air in the bottle? How does this compare to what solar energy does to air near the ground?

2. When the matches went out, the air inside the bottle cooled and contracted, creating lower pressure inside the bottle than outside the bottle. Describe how you think this impacted the egg.

3. Why do you think the egg would not come out of the bottle in Step 4?

4. Why do you think blowing into the bottle helped to get the egg back out?

The Impact of the Sun

Skill:

Write informative/explanatory text to convey concepts.

Describe how solar energy impacts the three elements of weather: temperature, wind, and precipitation. What do you think would happen to weather on Earth if we did not receive solar energy?

Climate

 ISBN: 9781925726558

An **electrical circuit** is the path of wires that allows electrons to flow through, in order to create electricity.

A simple electric circuit consists of a power source such as a battery, a device that will use the power such as a light bulb, and wires to connect them. A battery gives the force (voltage) that makes the electrons move.

Our world is full of circuits. They are used for millions of different purposes such as lighting our homes, opening the garage door, traffic lights or running a computer.

An electric **current** is the movement of **electrons** which flow through a circuit to power devices.

When a wire is connected to each end of a battery, electrons begin to flow from **negative to positive**.

When a circuit is **closed**, current can move from a battery through the wires, to the bulb and back to the battery because there is a path to follow.

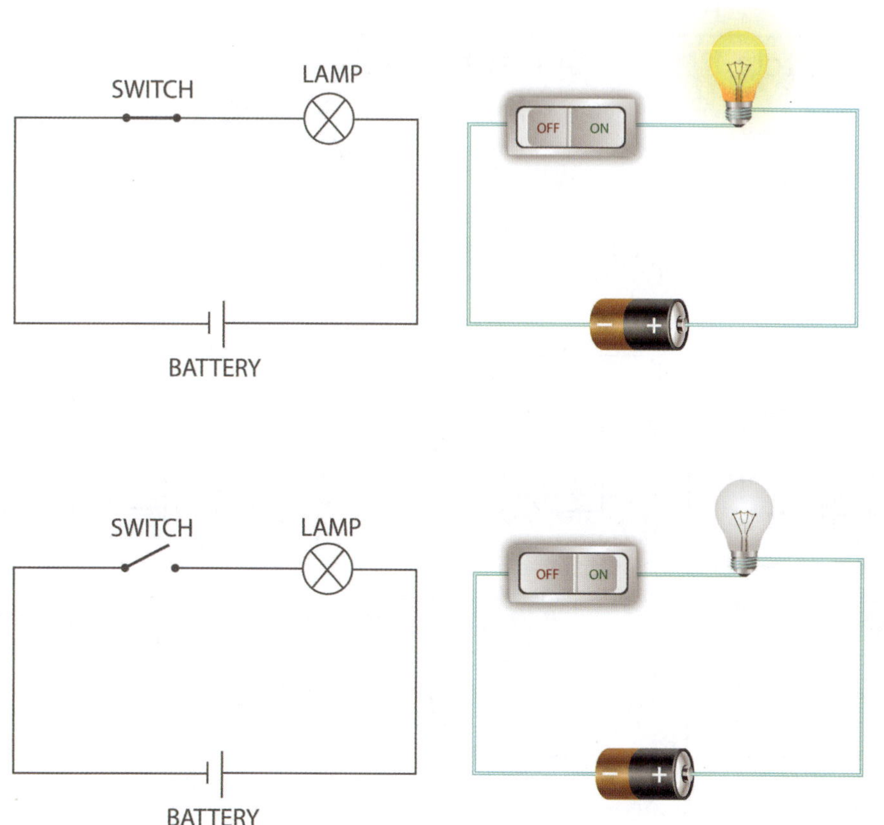

Electric Circuits

If there is a break in the circuit we say it is **open**, and the current cannot flow, because the path is not complete.

When there is a switch in the circuit and the switch is **off** it makes a gap and the current will **stop flowing**.

When the switch is **on**, it closes the gap and the electrons are able to **flow** and make the device work.

A circuit diagram is a map of a circuit. The purpose of the diagram is to use circuit symbols instead of drawing each component in the circuit. Scientists and electricians use these diagrams.

Can you colour match the component, purpose and symbol?

Component	Purpose	Circuit diagram symbol
Battery	Turns electricity to light	
Bulb	Opens and closes the circuit	
Wire	Starts electrical current	
Switch	Current travels along this	

Put a tick if you think the bulb will light up. Put a cross if you think it will not light up.

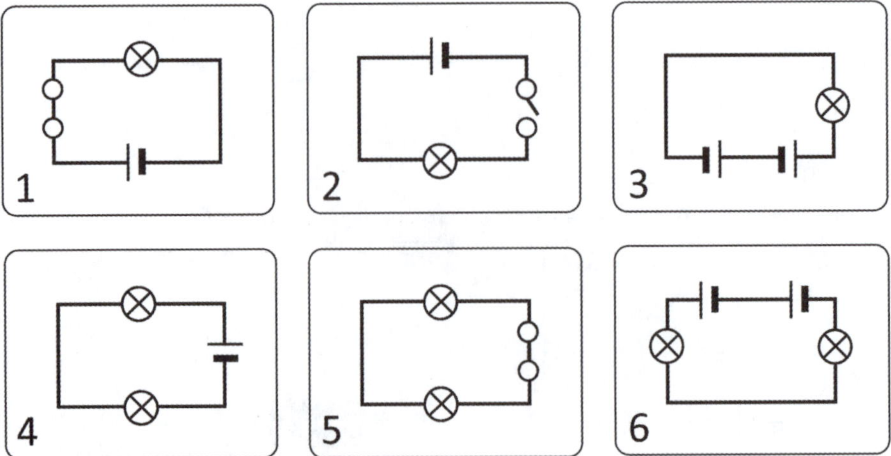

TARGETING SCIENCE YEAR 6 © PASCAL PRESS ISBN: 9781925726558

Series and Parallel Circuits

Series and **parallel** circuits are the two main types of electric circuits that can be found in electrical devices.

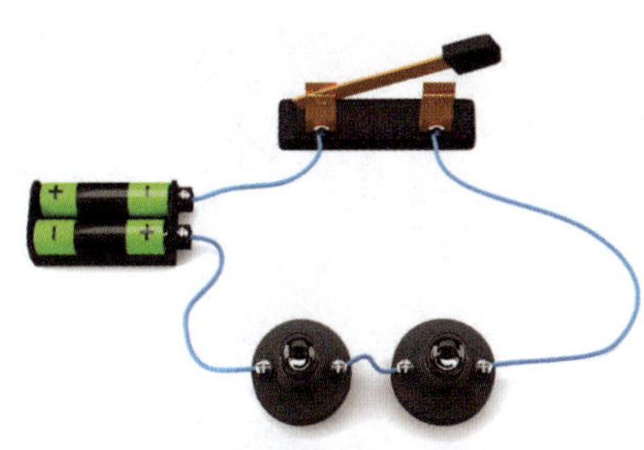

When electricity has only one path to follow, and every part is connected one after the other, or in a 'series', it is called a **series** circuit. There are no alternative pathways in a series circuit. A good way to remember is to think of a series you might enjoy watching on television - one episode follows on from another in a certain order.

Electrons flow from one end of the battery (also called a cell), along a path through the **resistors**, to the other end of the battery (the ends of the battery are called terminals). A resistor is anything that uses some of the power from the battery. Light bulbs, buzzers and motors are all examples of resistors.

If you were to take out, or damage any bulb in a series circuit, the entire circuit will not function because the path will be cut off and the electricity will not flow. Christmas lights used to be a great example of a series circuit. If one of the bulbs broke or stopped working, the whole length of lights stopped working. One advantage is that you will always know if there is a break in a series circuit. Now, with LED lights, the electrons can still follow a path to keep working, because there is no filament like there used to be in the old-style bulbs. Also, the more bulbs you add to the circuit, the dimmer the lights will be because many resistors are acting on the same voltage of power from the battery.

In a **parallel circuit**, there are many different pathways the electrons can follow. Since the electricity has more than one route to take, the circuit will still work even if one path fails. This is the reason why parallel circuits are more common. Your home is full of parallel circuits. Think of the light bulb in your bedroom. If it burns out, the light bulb in the kitchen and the rest of the house will not be affected. The great thing about parallel circuits is that no matter how many light bulbs you add, the lights will still shine bright without getting dimmer. The main benefit of using a parallel circuit is that it is useful if you want everything to work even if one component has failed.

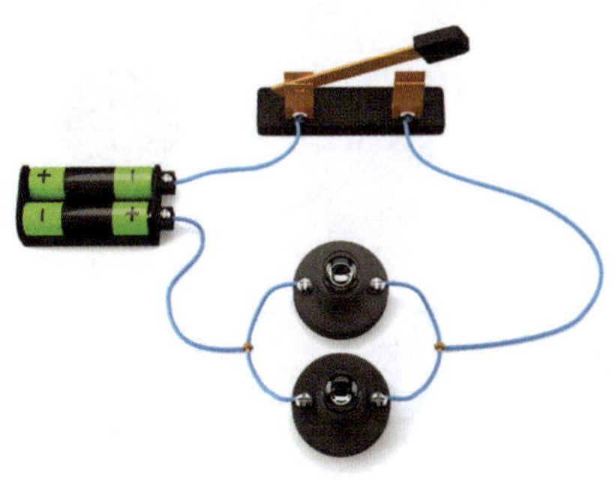

Series circuit advantages:	Series circuit disadvantages:	Parallel circuit advantages:	Parallel circuit disadvantages:

Conductors and Insulators

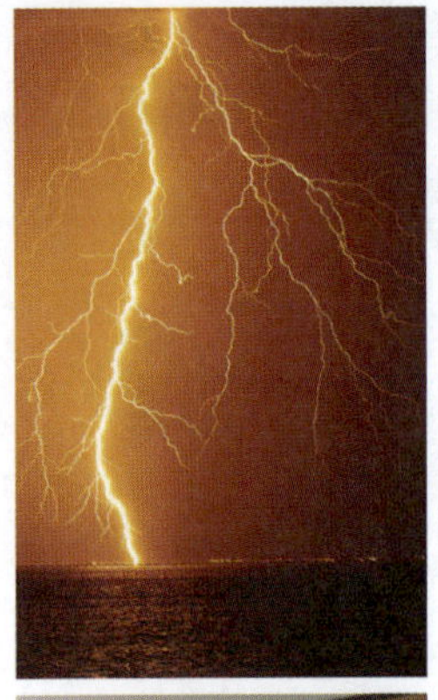

Conductors are materials that let electricity pass through them easily. Examples of conductors are metals such as steel, copper, iron and silver. Water is also a conductor, so anything that contains water also allows electricity to flow through it. This includes things like people, plants and animals.

Ever been told to get out of the water when there is a thunderstorm coming? It's because electrical storms involve **lightning**. Lightning is a giant spark of electricity in the atmosphere between the clouds, the air or the ground. If it struck the water it would travel through your body, because you are a good conductor of electricity.

Electricity passes through any conductor to reach the earth. If a person is the easiest route, the person will be **electrocuted**.

In a light bulb, the metal filament is a conductor and when the electrons flow through it, it causes the bulb to light up.

The copper wires in this image are surrounded by plastic insulation. This stops the electrons from escaping.

Insulators are materials that **do not** allow electricity to pass through them. This is generally because they have low or no water or metal content.

Plastic, glass, wood, and rubber are good examples of insulators. They are used to cover materials that carry electricity such as the plastic covering that surrounds wires.

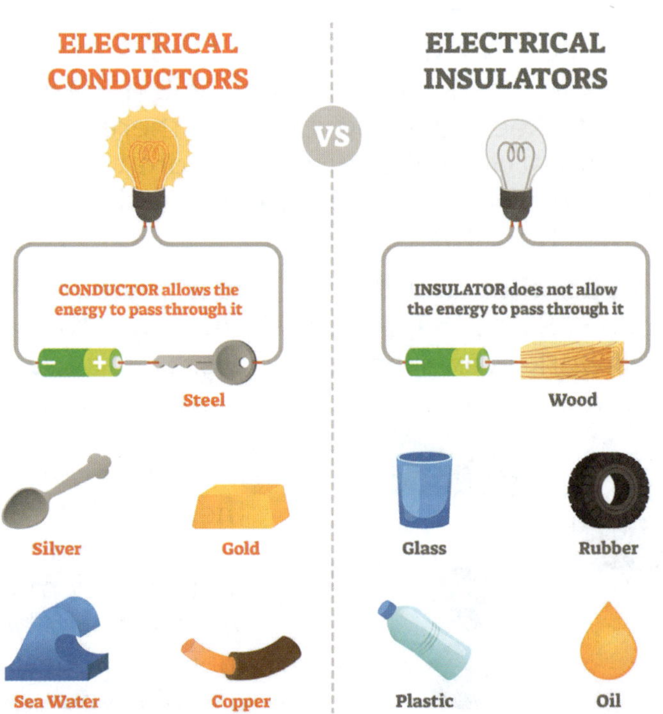

Make a list of the things around you that you think would be conductors and insulators. Remember... if it contains metal or water, it's probably going to be a conductor.

Conductors	Insulators

TARGETING SCIENCE YEAR 6 © PASCAL PRESS ISBN: 9781925726558

Define It!

digital: showing time by displaying numerals (digits)

display: information shown on a screen

LED: a type of light used in many devices

segment: one part of something that has been divided

Concepts:

Electric current creates light.

An LED display has bulbs in an electrical circuit.

Long ago, people lit fires when night fell. Today we can flip a switch and electricity will travel through a circuit to give us light. An **LED** is one type of light. LEDs are all around us. For example, they form the lighted numbers on **digital** clocks. An LED is a tiny light bulb that fits into an electrical circuit. Each clock number is divided into seven parts, or **segments**. Each segment is an LED that is connected separately to the circuit. When one of the LEDs receives electric current, that segment lights up. The time displayed on the clock changes as segments are turned on and off. For example, when all seven of the LED segments in a number are turned on, the **display** shows the number *8*. The clock has a counter that tells it when to change numbers and display the correct time.

Write *true* or *false*.

1. When electric current passes through an LED, sound is produced. ____________

2. An LED display uses segments that light up. ____________

The Electric Toaster

Concepts:

A circuit is a closed path through which electricity can flow.

Electric current causes heat.

Define It!

circuit: a closed path or loop through which electricity can flow

filament: a fine wire

lever: a bar used to operate a machine

resistor: something that limits the flow of electric current

An electric toaster is not as simple as it looks. When you push the **lever** down on a toaster, a switch completes a **circuit**. This sends electric current flowing through the toaster. Electric current flowing through a circuit can turn into heat. Inventors had a hard time figuring out how to make a toaster that wouldn't catch fire! They knew that electricity flows through conductors, such as metal. They also knew that some metals were not as good at conducting heat as others. Those metals are called **resistors**.

The glowing, red-hot **filaments** inside a toaster are resistors. The problem was how to keep the filaments from melting or burning. Albert Marsh solved the problem. He created a wire from two metals: nickel and chromium (KROH-me-uhm). The wire was a good resistor and could stand up to very high heat. This type of wire is still used in toasters today.

Complete the sentences.

1. A filament is a type of ________________.

2. Electric current flows through a toaster when the ________________ is complete.

Energy and Electricity

TARGETING SCIENCE YEAR 6 © PASCAL PRESS ISBN: 9781925726558

Converting Electrical Energy

Concept: Electrical energy can be converted into other forms of energy.

Define It!

filaments: wires that heat up or glow when they conduct electricity

mechanical energy: the sum of potential and kinetic energy; the energy of position and motion

All forms of energy can change into other forms. In a fireworks display, chemical energy becomes light and sound energy. When you cook popcorn, thermal energy turns into **mechanical energy**, which makes the popcorn jump. Electrical energy can also be converted into other forms of energy.

Think about the energy changes that take place when you toast a slice of bread. When you press down the switch on the toaster, you complete the circuit and send electrical energy through the wires to the **filaments** inside the toaster. There, the electrical energy converts into thermal energy, which heats the bread. If you look inside the toaster, you can see that the filaments glow. That's because some of the electrical energy has also changed into light energy.

Write *true* or *false*.

1. Electrical energy can only be converted to light energy. __________
2. Your bread toasts when electrical energy changes into thermal energy. __________
3. All energy can change into other forms of energy. __________

Time for Toast

Skill:

Label images that represent scientific concepts.

In a toaster that is turned on, electricity moves from the cord through the filaments to the switch and back out the cord. Label the *switch* and *filaments*. Then draw the path that the electric current travels through the toaster. Finally, explain what happens to the electric current when the toast pops up and why it happens.

TARGETING SCIENCE YEAR 6 © PASCAL PRESS ISBN: 9781925726555

Apply What You Learned

What is the science behind your breakfast toast? Explain how a toaster works step by step. Use the words *filament, lever, circuit,* and *resistor*. Then make a drawing and label it.

Draw

Skills:

Write explanatory text to convey information clearly.

Make a drawing and label it.

Vocabulary Practice

Select from the vocabulary words to complete the crossword puzzle.

mechanical energy	electrical energy	conductor	circuit	filaments
electric current	static electricity	switch	electron	insulator

Across

5. a material that does not permit the flow of electric current
6. wires that heat up or glow when they conduct electricity
7. a small particle with a negative charge

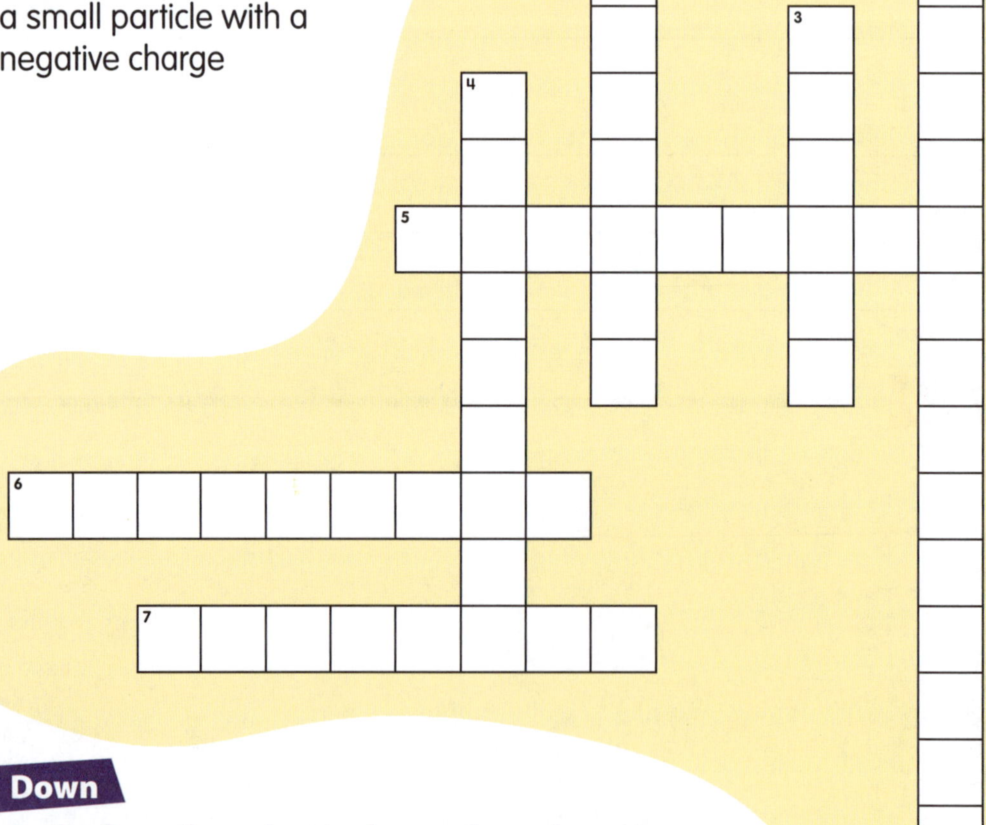

Down

1. the flow of an electric charge through a wire
2. a continuous path through which electricity flows
3. a part of a circuit that starts or stops the flow of electricity
4. a material that permits the flow of electric current

TARGETING SCIENCE YEAR 6 © PASCAL PRESS ISBN: 9781925726558

There's no doubt that electricity plays a very important role in our lives. **Electrical energy** provides power to devices old and new—from toasters and hearing aids to LED lights and electric cars. Electrical energy, or electricity, is the energy produced by the movement of electrons between atoms.

Electrical energy can occur in nature. Lightning is a form of electrical energy, as is **static electricity**, which is an electric charge that builds up on an object that has gained or lost **electrons**. You may have felt static electricity as a small shock to your finger or pieces of clothing that stick to your legs. However, these forms of electricity are temporary and difficult to control. The electrical energy that we use to power our devices is called **electric current**. This current is easier to control and can be made to flow through wires.

Define It!

electrical energy: energy produced by the movement of electrons between atoms

electric current: the flow of electricity, often through a wire

electron: a small particle in an atom that has a negative charge

static electricity: an electric charge that builds up on an object that has gained or lost electrons

Concepts:

Electrical energy is the energy produced by the movement of electrons between atoms.

Electricity exists as electric current or static electricity.

1. What is electrical energy?

____

____

2. What is the difference between static electricity and electric current?

____

____

____

____

____

Static Electricity

Skills:

Conduct experiments and draw conclusions about results.

In this experiment, you will create static electricity that you can see, feel, and hear!

Materials

- foam dinner plate
- foam cup
- piece of wool cloth
- disposable aluminium pie pan
- masking tape
- small plastic container with a plastic lid
- nail (slightly longer than the plastic container)
- aluminium foil
- water

Directions

1. Tape the top of the foam cup to the middle of the pie pan.

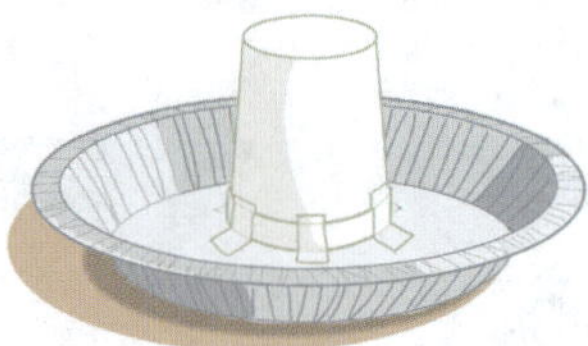

2. Push the nail through the centre of the lid of the plastic container. Wrap aluminium foil around the bottom two-thirds of the container.
3. Fill the plastic container almost to the top with water. Secure the lid. The nail should touch the water.

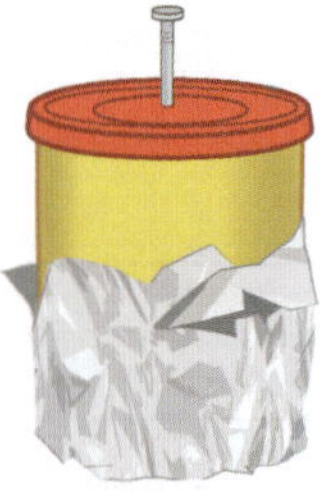

4. Rub the foam dinner plate with the wool cloth for a full minute. Place the plate upside down on a flat surface.
5. Place the pie pan on top of the plate. Briefly touch the pie pan with your finger. Record your observations on page 85.
6. Turn off the lights and close the shades. Remove the pie pan from the plate by holding the cup. You may have to hold the plate down with your other hand. Keep the pie pan at least 30 cm away from the plate.
7. Touch the pie pan again. Record your observations.
8. Place the pie pan back on the plate for 30 seconds to recharge it. With one hand, pick up the pie pan by the cup. Using the other hand, pick up the plastic container. Touch the nail to the pie pan and then put the pie pan down.
9. Put the plastic container down. Touch the aluminium foil with one finger and the tip of the nail with another finger. Record your observations.

TARGETING SCIENCE YEAR 6 © PASCAL PRESS ISBN: 9781925726558

	Observations
1st touch: pie pan	
2nd touch: pie pan	
3rd touch: plastic container	

What Did You Discover?

1. What happened when you first touched the pie pan?

____

2. What happened the second time you touched the pan? How was it different from the first time?

____

____

____

3. What happened when you touched the plastic container? How was it different from the times you touched the pie pan?

____

____

____

4. What gave the plate, pie pan, and plastic container their electric charge?

____

Electric Bills

Skills:

Collect, record, and analyse information.

We use electricity every day to power the devices in our homes. Make a list of all the items in your home that you think use electricity—from the lights to the TV to the air conditioning and/or heating. Then ask your parents to see the electric bills from four different months throughout the year; one for each season. Compare the bills to see when your bill was the most expensive. Try to determine why the electricity bill was more expensive during certain months. What are some things you can do to cut down on electricity usage? Devise a plan to conserve on your electric bill for next month.

List of Electric Devices in Home

____

____

____

____

____

____

Electric Bill Month: ______________________ **Cost:** $______________

Electric Bill Month: ______________________ **Cost:** $______________

Electric Bill Month: ______________________ **Cost:** $______________

Electric Bill Month: ______________________ **Cost:** $______________

In which month did you spend the most on electricity? Why do you think that happened?

____

____

What can you do to conserve energy and bring down the amount for next month's bill?

____

____

TARGETING SCIENCE YEAR 6 © PASCAL PRESS ISBN: 9781925726558

Electrical Energy Crossword Puzzle

Skill:
Apply content vocabulary.

Use the vocabulary words to complete the crossword puzzle.

hydroelectricity	turbine	display	filament
segment	digital	resistor	circuit

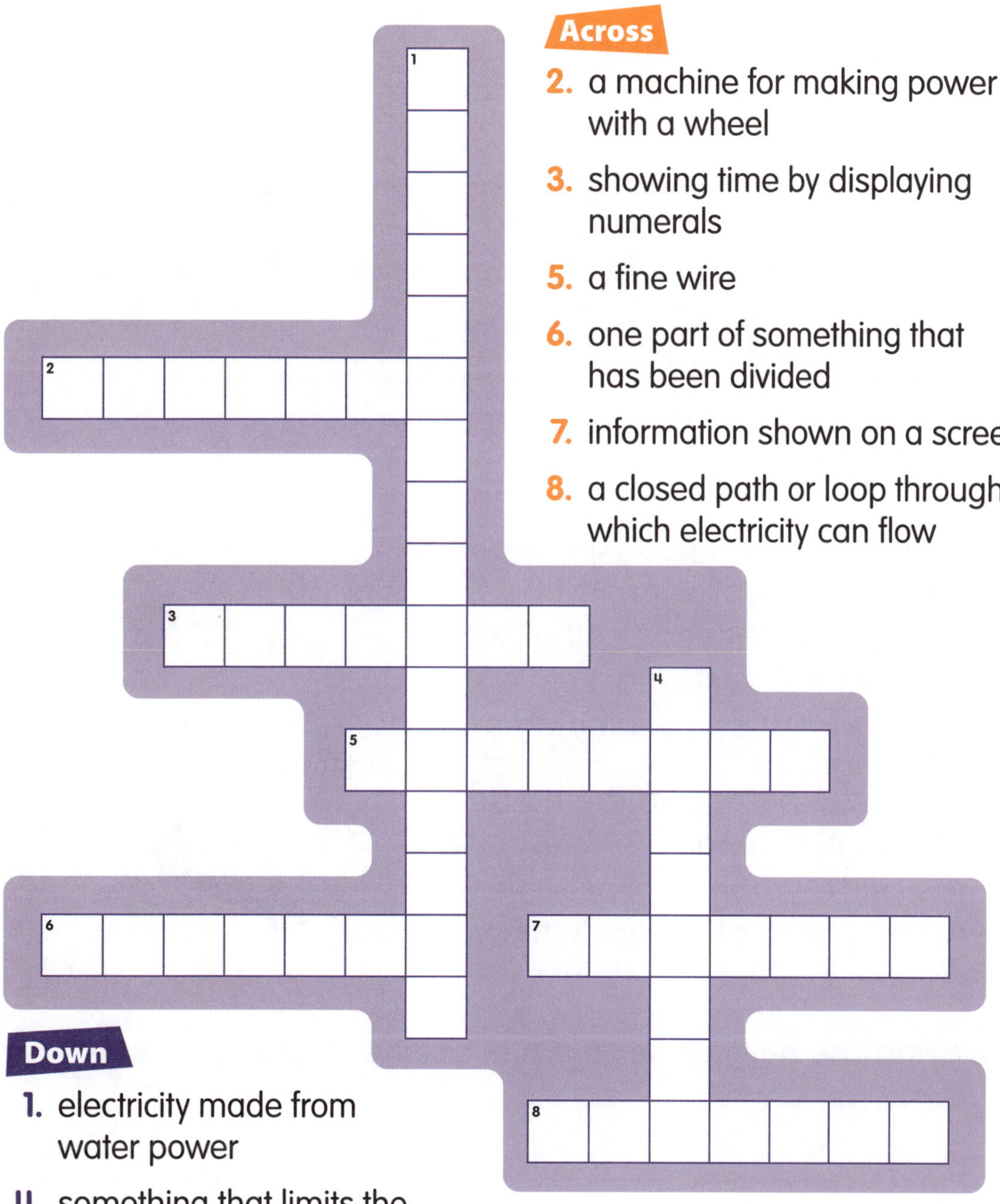

Across

2. a machine for making power with a wheel
3. showing time by displaying numerals
5. a fine wire
6. one part of something that has been divided
7. information shown on a screen
8. a closed path or loop through which electricity can flow

Down

1. electricity made from water power
4. something that limits the flow of electric current

An Electromagnet

Skills:

Follow a sequence of directions to conduct a science investigation.

Record observations and interpret results.

Electromagnets are used in electric motors. Many of the things you use every day have electromagnets—from doorbells to computers. You can demonstrate that a wire with electric current running through it creates a magnetic field. Make your own electromagnet!

What You Need

- 1.5 volt (AA) battery
- battery holder with clips
- 4 iron nails
- long insulated wire with stripped ends
- paper clips
- tape

Directions

1. Tape four iron nails together. Then wrap 10 coils of wire around the nails. Make sure that each coil of wire touches the next one. Leave some loose wire at the beginning and end.

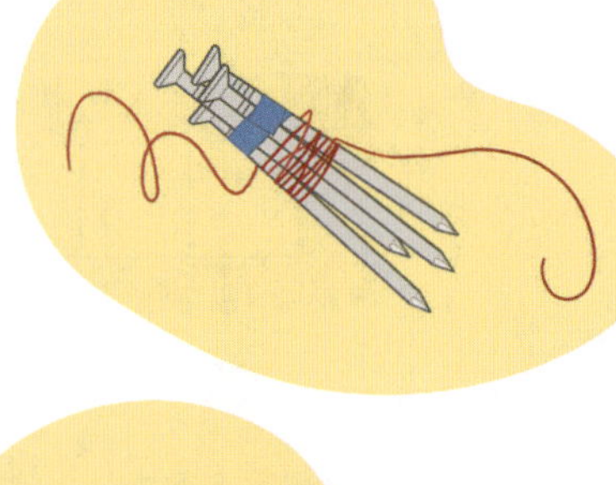

2. Place the battery in the holder. Attach both ends of the wire to the battery holder clips. This will make a circuit through which electric current can flow.

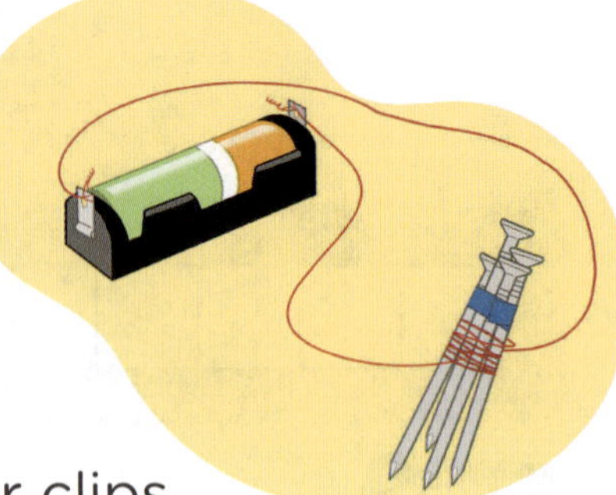

3. Bring the nails close to a pile of paper clips. What happens?

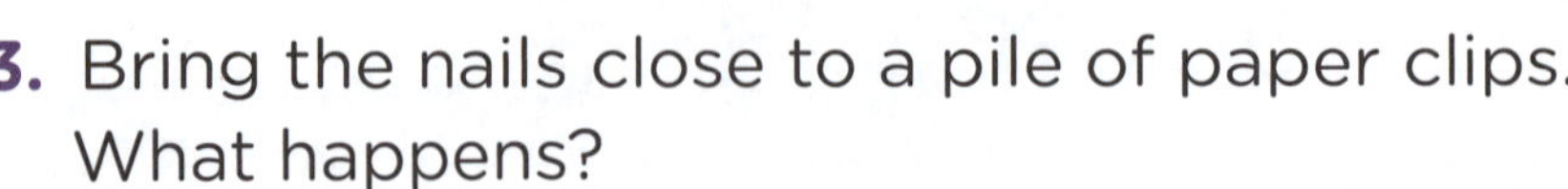

Energy and Electricity

TARGETING SCIENCE YEAR 6 © PASCAL PRESS ISBN: 9781925726558

4. In the chart, record the number of paper clips that were affected by 10 coils.

Number of Coils of Wire	Number of Paper Clips Affected
10	
20	
30	
40	

5. Wrap the wire around the nails 10 more times. How many paper clips do the nails pick up now? Record the number.

6. Repeat Step 5 two more times, each time adding 10 more coils.

Important **Note:** Do not leave the circuit connected for very long, as it could cause the circuit to fail and the battery to die.

7. How did the number of coils of wire around the nails affect the strength of the electromagnet?

____

____

Electrical Safety

Look at each of the pictures and answer YES or NO if you think they would be safe to do and explain why:

Victoria touches a powerpoint with wet hands.
Yes or No?
Why?

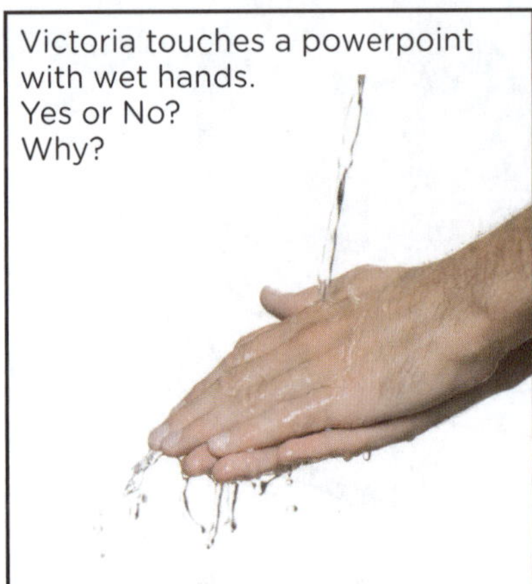

Carly looks to see there are no powerlines before she flies her kite?
Yes or No?
Why?

Jeremy pulls out the cable by the cord.
Yes or No?
Why?

Owen hides under a tree in thunderstorm.
Yes or NO?
Why?

Anwar decides to save time and fix the cable himself.
Yes or No?
Why?

The kids get out of the pool before the storm hits.
Yes or No?
Why?

Sophia blowdries her hair when her little sister is in the bath.
Yes or No?
Why?

Bella moves her drink away from the computer.
Yes or No?
Why?

Claudia digs a hole for a tree under the powerpole.
Yes or No?
Why?

David's dad turns the power off before he changes the lightbulb.
Yes or No?
Why?

Sam tells his baby brother not to put anything in the powerpoint. He tells his mum what he saw.
Yes or No?
Why?

Barney uses a knife to get burnt toast out of the toaster.
Yes or No?
Why?

TARGETING SCIENCE YEAR 6 © PASCAL PRESS ISBN: 9781925726558

The universe runs on **energy**. We use energy for everything we do, from swimming laps in the pool to turning on the lights— even for growing and thinking! Scientists define energy as the ability to do work.

https://clickv.ie/w/Fxgx

Use this QR code to access a video on this topic.

Define It!

electron: a negatively charged particle found in atoms

energy: the ability to do work

kinetic energy: the energy of motion

potential energy: stored energy due to position or condition

vibrations: a series of small, fast movements back and forth

Energy comes in many different forms. These include electrical energy, thermal energy, mechanical energy, and chemical energy. Electrical energy, or electricity, is energy produced by the movement of **electrons** between atoms. Thermal energy is internal energy produced by the **vibrations** of an object's molecules. Mechanical energy is the energy of a movable object. And chemical energy is energy contained in chemical bonds of molecules. Each of these forms of energy exists in two types: **kinetic energy**, or the energy of motion, and **potential energy**, or stored energy.

electrical

thermal

mechanical

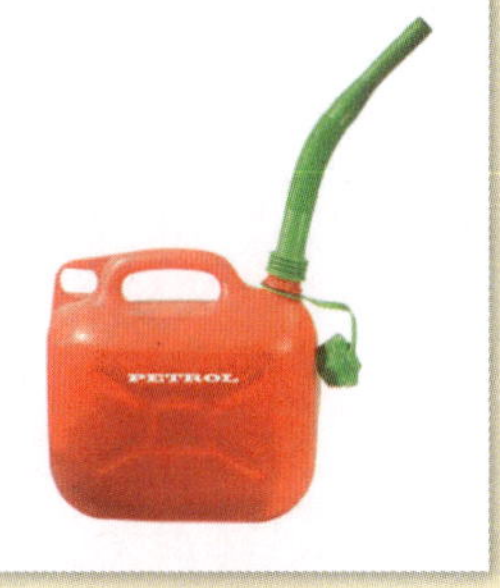

chemical

Complete the sentences.

1. Electricity is ___________________ energy.
2. The energy produced by a movable object is called ___________________ energy.
3. Stored energy is also called ___________________ energy.
4. The energy contained in the chemical bonds of molecules is

   ___________________ energy.

Concepts:

Energy is the ability to do work.

There are many types of energy.

Kinds of Energy

Skills:

Interpret and apply information gained from text and illustrations.

Electric currents can move energy from place to place. Electric currents produce heat energy in a toaster and light energy in an LED. They also produce the energy of motion in a fan and the energy of sound in a microphone.

For each picture, list one or more kinds of energy that are being produced from electric currents. Use the words *heat, light, motion,* and *sound*.

Energy and Electricity

TARGETING SCIENCE YEAR 6 © PASCAL PRESS ISBN: 9781925726558

Kinetic Energy

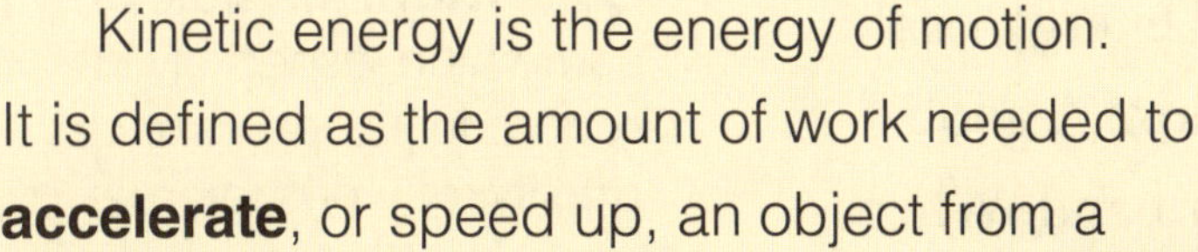

Kinetic energy is the energy of motion. It is defined as the amount of work needed to **accelerate**, or speed up, an object from a resting state to one of movement. For example, a cyclist uses the chemical energy provided by food to pedal his bike. That chemical energy is **converted** to kinetic energy as the cyclist speeds up. The faster an object moves, the more kinetic energy it has. A cyclist moving at 10 km/h has more kinetic energy than a cyclist moving at 5 km/h. Once an object gains kinetic energy during its acceleration, it maintains the same amount of energy unless its speed changes.

Define It!

accelerate: to speed up

convert: to change into

Rena Schild / Shutterstock.com

Kinetic energy can be passed from one object to another. For example, in the game of pool, kinetic energy is transferred from the cue stick to the ball. If that ball hits another ball, its kinetic energy will transfer to the second ball. As a result, the first ball slows down and the second ball accelerates.

Describe how kinetic energy can be passed from one object to another in a game of pool.

____

____

____

____

Concepts:

Kinetic energy is the energy of motion.

Kinetic energy can be passed from one object to another.

Potential Energy

Concepts:

Potential energy is stored energy.

Energy can be changed from one form to another.

Define It!

condition: the state of something, especially in regard to its appearance, quality, or working order

incline: a slope or rise

transform: to dramatically change in form, appearance, or character

Potential energy is stored energy, or the energy of position or **condition**. A good example is a stretched rubber band. When the rubber band is stretched, potential energy is stored in it. When the rubber band is released, the potential energy is converted to kinetic energy as the rubber band snaps back. Another good example of potential energy is a lawn mower filled with petrol or a car at the top of a hill. Potential energy is essentially energy that is ready to be used.

Energy can be changed from one form to another. As a roller coaster car races down the track, its potential energy is converted into kinetic energy. Once the car begins to climb back up the **incline**, the kinetic energy is then converted back to potential energy. Although energy can change form and be transferred from one object to another, the total amount of energy in a system remains constant. Energy cannot be created or destroyed—only **transformed**. In physics, this is called *the law of conservation of energy*.

Chris Parypa Photography / Shutterstock.com

Write *true* or *false*.

1. Energy cannot be created or destroyed. __________
2. Energy cannot change from one form to another. __________
3. A stretched rubber band is an example of kinetic energy. __________

Potential or Kinetic?

Skill:

Label images that represent scientific concepts.

Look at the pictures below. Label whether the picture shows *potential energy* or *kinetic energy*.

____

____

____

____

____

Energy and Electricity

Transfer of Energy

Skill:

Write informative/explanatory text to convey concepts.

Make a list of two physical activities you have done or will do today. Examples include walking to the bus stop, lifting an object, playing cricket, or riding a bike. Think about which parts of your physical activities represent *potential energy,* and which parts represent *kinetic energy*. Describe how the energy changes form in each of your activities. Then write down whether any kinetic energy is transferred from one object to another during your activities.

Activity 1

____

____

____

____

____

____

____

Activity 2

____

____

____

____

____

____

____

TARGETING SCIENCE YEAR 6 © PASCAL PRESS ISBN: 9781925726558

https://clickv.ie/w/c0gx

Use this QR code to access a video on this topic.

Define It!

generator: a machine that produces electricity

hydroelectricity: electricity made from water power

rotor: part of a machine that turns

shaft: a long rod used in a machine

turbine: a machine with a wheel for making power

Most electricity in the Australia is made by power plants that burn natural gas, coal, and oil. But a small amount of the electricity we use comes from wind. Wind **turbines** change the kinetic energy of wind into electrical energy. Wind turns the giant turbine blades. The blades turn a **rotor** that turns a **shaft**. The shaft spins a **generator** that makes electric current. The electric current travels through wires to homes, schools, and other places.

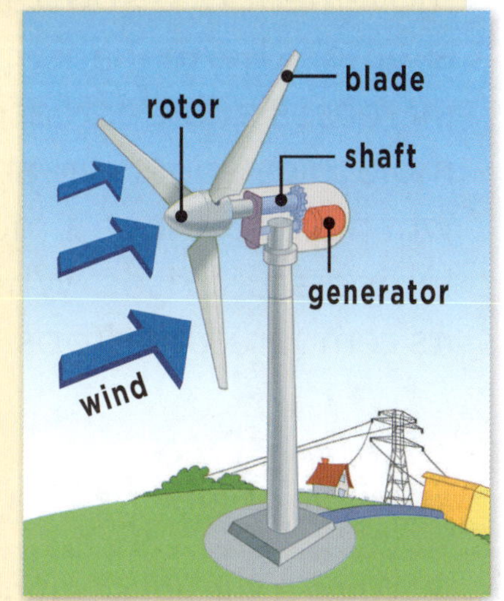

Another small part of the electricity produced comes from the power of moving water. This is called **hydroelectricity**. (*Hydro* means "water.") Water falling over a dam has enough force to spin the blades of giant turbines. The energy of the turbines is changed into electricity.

Concepts:

Turbines change kinetic energy of wind and water into electrical energy.

Hydro-electricity is created from the power of water.

Write the answers.

1. What changes the kinetic energy of wind to electric current?

____

2. What changes the kinetic energy of water to electric current?

____

What Is Thermal Energy?

Concepts:

Thermal energy is energy produced by the movement and attractions of molecules within a substance.

Temperature is the measure of a substance's average thermal energy.

The molecules that make up a substance are in constant motion. This motion produces an **internal** energy. The internal energy of a substance, produced by the vibrations and attractions of its molecules, is called **thermal energy**. We use thermal energy to heat our homes and cook our food.

https://clickv.ie/w/Mxgx

Use this QR code to access a video on this topic.

Define It!

generate: to produce something

internal: situated on the inside

temperature: a measure of the average thermal energy of the molecules of a substance

thermal energy: energy produced by the movement and attractions of molecules within a substance

When we measure **temperature**, we are measuring the average energy **generated** by the movement of a substance's molecules, or its average thermal energy. Thermal energy increases and decreases as a substance's molecules speed up and slow down. Therefore, when a substance's molecules speed up, its temperature rises. When its molecules slow down, its temperature drops.

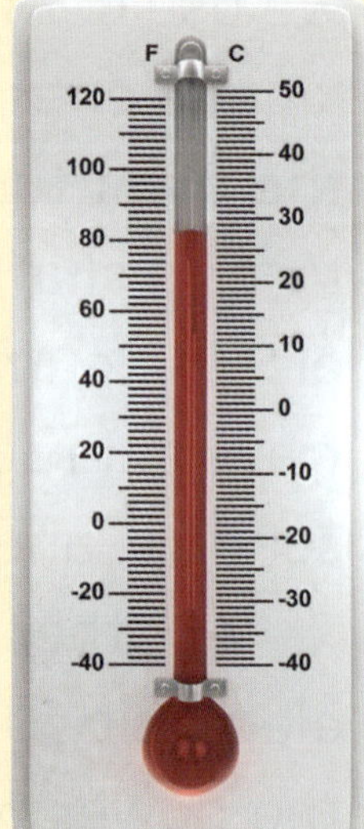

Write *true* or *false*.

1. When a substance's molecules slow down, its temperature increases. __________

2. When a substance's molecules speed up, its thermal energy increases. __________

3. The internal energy of a substance is called its temperature. __________

4. Thermal energy is produced by the vibrations and attractions of a substance's molecules. __________

TARGETING SCIENCE YEAR 6 © PASCAL PRESS ISBN: 9781925726558

Define It!

heat: the transfer of thermal energy

Any change in matter requires energy. For example, we need thermal energy to cook popcorn. When popcorn is cooked, its thermal energy increases. We see this change in thermal energy when the popcorn transforms from kernels into fluffy white puffs. We feel this change in thermal energy as **heat**.

Although we experience thermal energy as heat, the two are different. Heat is the **transfer** of thermal energy. Heat always flows from objects with more thermal energy to those with less energy. When an object feels warm to the touch, it is because the object has more thermal energy than your fingertips do. When heat flows from the object to your fingers, you feel this gain of thermal energy as warmth. When an object feels cold, it is because the object has less thermal energy than your fingertips do. As heat flows from your fingertips to the object, you feel this loss of thermal energy as cold.

More thermal energy → Heat transfer → Less thermal energy

When we increase the thermal energy of popcorn by cooking it, we can sense very clear changes. We **see** the popcorn change from a kernel into a white puff. We **feel** the warmth of the heated popcorn. In what other way do you think we can sense the change in popcorn's thermal energy?

____

____

____

Concepts:

Heat and thermal energy are not the same thing.

Heat is the transfer of thermal energy from a warmer object to a cooler one.

Three Ways Heat Is Transferred

Concept:

Conduction transfers heat through physical contact, convection through the movement of a liquid or gas, and radiation through waves that move through matter or empty space.

Define It!

conduction: the transfer of thermal energy by physical contact

convection: the transfer of thermal energy through the movement of a liquid or gas

radiation: the transfer of thermal energy by waves that move through matter or empty space

Heat is the flow of thermal energy from warmer objects to cooler objects. Heat moves between objects of different temperatures in a variety of ways.

If you warm your hands on a hot cup of cocoa, heat flows from the cup to your hands by means of **conduction**. Conduction is the transfer of thermal energy through physical contact. When you hold your hands by a fire, waves of energy from the flames transfer heat to your hands by means of **radiation**. Radiation is the movement of energy waves through matter or empty space. Finally, drying your hands under a hot-air dryer warms them by **convection**. Convection is the transfer of thermal energy through the movement of a liquid or gas.

Microwave ovens cook food by means of radiation.

These eggs are fried by means of conduction.

Water boils by means of convection.

Name and describe the three ways heat is transferred.

____

____

____

____

____

TARGETING SCIENCE YEAR 6 © PASCAL PRESS ISBN: 9781925726558

Conduction, Convection, and Radiation

Skill:

Label images that represent scientific concepts.

The picture below shows three examples of heat being transferred through *conduction*, *convection*, and *radiation*. Label where each of these is taking place. Then explain how conduction, convection, and radiation are warming the objects in the picture.

Vocabulary Practice

Skill:

Apply content vocabulary.

Select from the vocabulary words to complete the sentences. Then unscramble the shaded letters to decode the secret message.

thermal energy	heat	conduction	generate
temperature	radiation	convection	internal

1. ___ ___ ___ ___ ___ ___ ___ ___ ___ is what cooks your food in a microwave oven.

2. When the molecules within a substance move, they ___ ___ ___ ___ ___ ___ ___ ___ energy.

3. ___ ___ ___ ___ is the transfer of ___ ___ ___ ___ ___ ___ ___ ___ ___ ___ ___ ___ ___ ___ from warmer objects to cooler ones.

4. When you take your ___ ___ ___ ___ ___ ___ ___ ___ ___ ___ ___, you are measuring the average amount of your thermal energy.

5. Thermal energy is also called ___ ___ ___ ___ ___ ___ ___ ___ energy.

6. When you fry an egg in a frying pan, you are cooking it by means of ___ ___ ___ ___ ___ ___ ___ ___ ___ ___.

___ ___ ___ ___ ___ ___ ___ ___ ___ ___ ___ ___ ___ ___ ___ ___ ___ ___ ___

waves from the sun warm Earth through radiation.

Energy and Electricity

TARGETING SCIENCE YEAR 6 © PASCAL PRESS ISBN: 9781925726558

Rubber Band Car

Skills: Conduct experiments and draw conclusions about results.

See potential and kinetic energy at work by building your own rubber band-powered car!

Materials

- 2 compact discs (CDs)
- 2 ½" cm tap washers
- 15 cm x 15 cm square of corrugated cardboard
- wooden skewer (as thin as possible)
- poster putty
- rubber bands of different sizes
- ruler
- scissors
- tape (masking or duct)

Directions

1. Hold the cardboard so that the corrugations (grooves) run horizontally left to right. Cut out a notch in the centre of one side of the cardboard as shown. The notch should be 5 cm wide by 3.8 cm deep.
2. Slide the skewer through one of the corrugations in the cardboard so that it runs across the notch as shown. Make sure the skewer has equal lengths on each side of the cardboard.
3. Wrap a piece of tape around the skewer in the centre of the notch. Create a tab with the tape to make a "catch" for the rubber band.
4. Place a washer in the centre of a CD. Slide the CD onto one of the skewers, leaving plenty of room between the "wheel" and the cardboard.

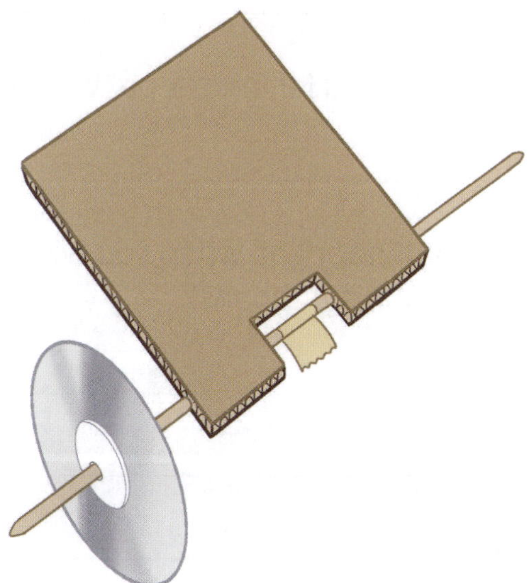

Rubber Band Car

5. Put poster putty on both sides of the washer to join the washer, CD, and skewer together very tightly. When you spin the CD, the skewer should spin with it.

6. Repeat Steps 4 and 5 to make the second wheel.

7. Choose a rubber band. Tape one end of the rubber band to the cardboard at the opposite end from the notch as shown.

8. Hook the unattached end of the rubber band over the catch on the skewer. Turn the skewer several times to tighten the rubber band.

9. Place the car on the ground, let go of the skewer, and watch it go!

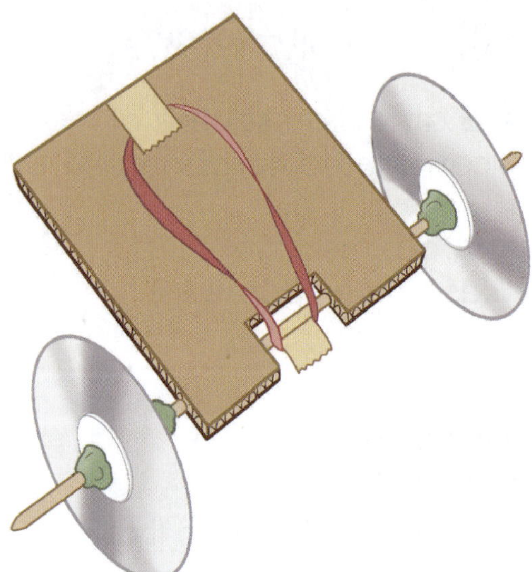

What Did You Discover?

1. When you wind up the skewer, what kind of energy does the car have?

____

2. When you let the car go, what kind of energy does it have?

____

3. What happens when you wind the rubber band even more? Why do you think this happens?

____

____

____

____

TARGETING SCIENCE YEAR 6 © PASCAL PRESS ISBN: 9781925726558

Skill: Apply content vocabulary.

Select from the vocabulary words to complete the crossword puzzle.

potential energy	energy	accelerate	convert	transform
kinetic energy	vibrations	condition	electron	incline

Across

7. the energy of motion
8. the state of something

Down

1. a series of small, fast movements
2. a negatively charged particle found in atoms
3. to dramatically change in form
4. to change into
5. the ability to do work
6. a rise

Mixtures

Concept:

A mixture is a combination of substances in which the structure of the substances does not change.

Mixtures are almost everywhere you look. In fact, most materials found in nature are mixtures. Sand is a mixture of rocks and broken shells, and soil is a mixture of dirt and **organic** materials—even the air is a mixture of different gases. A mixture is a combination of two or more different substances. When a mixture is combined, the substances go through a physical change, but the **structure** of the substances, or the way the molecules are organised, remains the same. Rocks and broken shells are still rocks and broken shells, even when they are mixed together in sand.

Some mixtures can be separated easily. You can pick out the individual pieces of fruit from a fruit salad, or separate the raisins from the nuts in a trail mix. However, other mixtures are much more difficult to "undo." For example, you could not easily separate the flour, butter, eggs, and sugar from cake batter after they've been mixed together.

Define It!

mixture: a combination of two or more substances in which the substances themselves are not changed

organic: living

structure: the way that molecules are organised in a substance

These are all different types of mixtures.

Complete the sentences.

1. Soil is a mixture of dirt and ________________ materials.
2. When substances are combined in a mixture, the ________________ of the substances does not change.
3. Substances in a mixture go through a ________________ change.

Chemistry

TARGETING SCIENCE YEAR 6 © PASCAL PRESS ISBN: 9781925726558

Some types of mixtures are blended together so well that you cannot see the substances' separate parts. A mixture in which all the parts are mixed evenly is called a **solution**. Salt water is a solution. If you put a tablespoon of salt in a glass of water, the salt mixes evenly with the water. No one part of the water will be saltier than another part.

A solution is made up of a **solute** and a **solvent**. A solute is the substance that **dissolves** in a solution. Salt, for example, is a solute. A solvent is the substance that it dissolves in. Water, for example, is a solvent. A solute is often a solid, but it can also be a liquid or a gas. A solvent is usually a liquid.

Define It!

dissolve: to mix, usually with a liquid, so that the substance is spread evenly throughout

solute: a substance dissolved in another substance

solution: a mixture of two or more substances in which all the parts are mixed evenly

solvent: a substance that dissolves another substance

Concepts:

A solution is a mixture in which all the parts are evenly mixed.

A solution is made up of a solute and a solvent.

Write which substances are *solutes* and which are *solvents* in the solutions below.

Fruit Punch

Fruit flavouring: ____________

Water: ____________

Sparkling Water

Water: ____________

Carbon dioxide: ____________

Chocolate Milk

Milk: ____________

Sugar: ____________

Cocoa: ____________

Solubility

Concepts:

Solubility is a substance's ability to dissolve.

Solubility is a physical property.

A substance's ability to dissolve is a kind of physical property called **solubility**. Many substances dissolve easily in water and other liquids. For example, the solubility of sugar is high because it dissolves well in water. Other substances are less soluble. For example, an aspirin can dissolve in a cup of water, but it takes a long time and often leaves **residue** at the bottom of the cup.

Not all substances are **soluble**. For example, oil does not dissolve in water. When you shake a bottle of salad dressing that contains oil, water, and vinegar, the liquids mix together only temporarily. After a while, the oil separates from the vinegar and water and floats to the top of the liquid mixture.

Define It!

residue: a small amount of something left over from the main part

solubility: the ability to dissolve

soluble: able to be dissolved

This table shows how soluble different substances are in water. The higher the number, the more soluble the substance is. Use this information to answer the questions.

	Solubility (per gram of water)
Oxygen	0.0000434 gram
Carbon dioxide	0.00145 gram
Sugar	2.0 grams
Salt	0.36 gram

1. Which substance dissolves best in water? ________________

2. Which gas dissolves more easily in water—oxygen or carbon dioxide? ________________

3. Which substance is the least soluble in water? ________________

TARGETING SCIENCE YEAR 6 © PASCAL PRESS ISBN: 9781925726558

Keep 'Em Separated

Skill:

Interpret information from graphic images.

Look at the three pictures of mixtures below. Number the pictures from easiest to separate to hardest to separate, *1* being the easiest and *3* being the hardest. Then explain why you ranked the pictures the way you did.

= ______

= ______

= ______

____

____

____

____

____

____

____

TARGETING SCIENCE YEAR 6 © PASCAL PRESS ISBN: 9781925726558

Vocabulary Practice

Skill:
Apply content vocabulary.

Select from the vocabulary words to complete the sentences. Then unscramble the shaded letters to decode the secret message.

dissolve	solubility	mixture	solvent	solution
structure	soluble	solute	organic	residue

1. A ___ ___ ___ ___ ___ ___ ___ is a combination of two or more substances.

2. In salt water, the salt is the ___ ___ ___ ___ ___ ___ and the water is the ___ ___ ___ ___ ___ ___ ___.

3. Aspirin is not as ___ ___ ___ ___ ___ ___ ___ in water as sugar is.

4. A ___ ___ ___ ___ ___ ___ ___ ___ is a combination of substances in which all the parts are blended evenly.

5. Soil is a mixture of dirt and ___ ___ ___ ___ ___ ___ ___ materials.

6. A substance's ___ ___ ___ ___ ___ ___ ___ ___ ___ ___, or ability to ___ ___ ___ ___ ___ ___ ___ ___, is a physical property.

Brass, pewter, bronze, and steel are mixtures of metal called ___ ___ ___ ___ ___ ___.

Chemistry

TARGETING SCIENCE YEAR 6 © PASCAL PRESS ISBN: 9781925726558

Skills:

Conduct experiments, analyse data, and record results.

In this activity, you will create four different mixtures. Then you will separate the mixtures using different methods for each substance.

What You Need

- 4 small clear cups, labeled **1**, **2**, **3**, **4**
- spoon
- salt
- sand
- gravel
- iron filings
- magnet
- strainer
- coffee filter
- warm water

Directions

1. Fill Cup 1 with warm water and add a spoonful of salt. Stir and watch what happens. Record your observations in the chart on page 112.
2. Fill Cup 2 with warm water and add a spoonful of sand. Stir and watch what happens. Record your observations.
3. Fill Cup 3 with warm water and add a spoonful of gravel. Stir and watch what happens. Record your observations.
4. Fill Cup 4 with warm water and add a spoonful of iron filings. Stir and watch what happens. Record your observations.
5. Leave Cup 1 in a well-lit window. Check back on the cup the next day. Record your observations.
6. For the other three mixtures (Cups 2–4), test which of the materials—the magnet, the strainer, or the coffee filter—is best for separating the substances.

	Description of mixture	How to separate
Cup 1		
Cup 2		
Cup 3		
Cup 4		

What Did You Discover?

1. Which of the mixtures is a solution? How do you know this?

2. What happened to the salt water after you left it in the window for a day?

3. Name some ways that you could completely separate the salt from the water.

4. Which materials were best for separating the other mixtures? Why?

TARGETING SCIENCE YEAR 6 © PASCAL PRESS ISBN: 9781925726558

Watch a parent, grandparent, or other adult make dinner. Observe how many of the dishes are **mixtures**. Write the ingredients of the mixtures. Then write whether you think the mixtures can be easily separated. Next, write the **solutions** that you are eating or drinking.

Skills: Make and record observations.

Mixture ______________________

Ingredients:

____
____
____
____
____

Ability to be separated:

____

Mixture ______________________

Ingredients:

____
____
____
____
____

Ability to be separated:

____

Solution ______________________

Ingredients:

____
____
____

Solution ______________________

Ingredients:

____
____
____

Chemistry

Physical Properties vs. Chemical Properties

Concepts:

Chemical properties describe a substance's ability to go through a chemical change.

All substances have both physical and **chemical properties**. Physical properties can be seen or measured. Physical properties include things such as colour, texture, and shape. Chemical properties, however, cannot be seen. Chemical properties describe a substance's **potential** to go through a **chemical change**. For example, hydrogen has the potential to **ignite** and explode under the right conditions.

Define It!

chemical change: a change in which one or more new substances are formed

chemical property: the potential of a substance to change into a different substance

ignite: to catch fire

potential: possibility; not yet completely developed

Although you cannot see chemical properties, you can observe how substances transform after they go through a chemical change. Clues that a chemical change has taken place include light, heat, colour change, odour, or sound. The light from hydrogen catching fire and the sound of the explosion are both signs of a chemical change. Unlike physical changes, chemical changes cannot be undone. When you toast a slice of bread, the toast cannot go back to being plain bread. Toasting bread is a type of chemical change.

Write *true* or *false*.

1. Chemical properties can be seen and measured. ____________
2. Physical changes can be undone. ____________
3. Chemical properties describe a substance's potential to change into another substance. ____________
4. Toasting bread is a physical change. ____________

Chemistry

TARGETING SCIENCE YEAR 6 © PASCAL PRESS ISBN: 9781925726558

Define It!

bond: the force that holds together the particles of a molecule

molecular: of or relating to molecules

product: a new substance that is formed during a chemical reaction

reactant: a substance that changes during a chemical reaction

Unlike a physical change where no new substances are created, a chemical change does create new substances. For example, when you boil water, the water vapour is still water. Boiling water is an example of a physical change. However, when you burn a piece of wood, the wood turns into ash. Burning wood is an example of a chemical change.

When a chemical change takes place, it happens at the **molecular** level. During a chemical change, the structures of the substances' molecules are altered. The **bonds** of the molecules are broken and re-formed to create new molecules. The new molecules are different from the molecules of the original substances.

Chemical changes are also called chemical reactions. In a chemical reaction, the original substances are called **reactants** and the new substances that they form are called **products**. For example, in the chemical reaction that forms rust, the reactants are iron and oxygen. The product they form when they interact with water is called iron oxide. The iron oxide product, like all products of a chemical reaction, has different properties from the iron and oxygen that formed it. Oxygen is a gas and iron is a strong silver metal. Iron oxide, or rust, is brownish-orange, and it crumbles easily.

Concepts: Chemical reactions change the structure of substances and create new sub-stances.

Answer the questions.

1. What are the reactants in the chemical reaction that forms rust? What is the product?

____

2. What is the difference between a physical change and a chemical change?

____

____

Conservation of Mass

Concepts:

In any chemical reaction, mass is neither created nor destroyed.

Whenever a substance goes through a chemical change, it becomes a different substance. However, it's important to understand that the total mass of the substance does not change. In **physics**, this is called the law of **conservation of mass**.

Define It!

conservation of mass: a principle that states that the total mass of any substance is not increased or decreased by a chemical reaction

physics: the science of matter and energy and their interactions

Law of Conservation of Mass

The law of conservation of mass states that in any chemical reaction, mass is neither created nor destroyed. It is only rearranged. The mass of the products equals the mass of the reactants.

For every particle that is lost by a substance in a chemical reaction, a particle is gained by another substance. In the case of rusting metal, particles from the iron molecules move to the oxygen molecules. This forms iron oxide, or rust. But the iron oxide product has the same number of particles as the iron and oxygen particles that began the reaction.

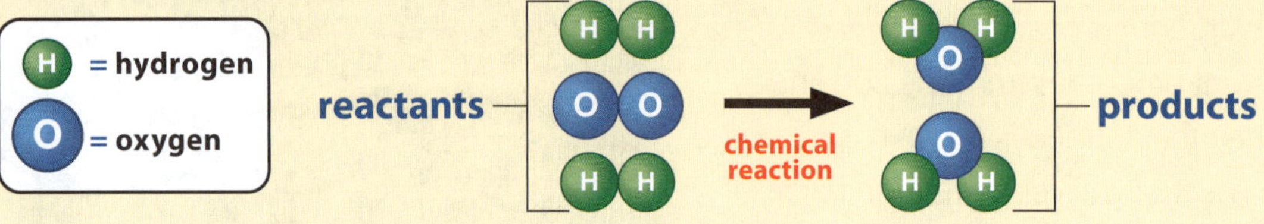

In the diagram above, **H** stands for *hydrogen* and **O** stands for *oxygen*. Use this information to answer the questions.

1. How many hydrogen particles are at the start of the chemical reaction? _____
2. How many hydrogen particles are at the end of the chemical reaction? _____
3. Is the number of oxygen particles the same before and after the chemical reaction? Explain why or why not.

____

____

____

Chemistry

TARGETING SCIENCE YEAR 6 © PASCAL PRESS ISBN: 9781925726558

Changes to Materials

In chemistry, most changes to materials can be broken into two groups: Physical Change and Chemical Change.

In a physical change, the material might change shape, size or the form it takes, but no new substance is made.

For example, you could cut a piece of fabric or a block of wood, and it would look different, but you have not made a new substance. It is a change in form, but not in composition.

You could melt an ice block so that it is now a liquid, but you have not made a new substance, just the form that it took.

Some physical changes can be reversed or undone, like re-freezing the ice, but it would be hard to make the wood pieces into a block again, even though it is still wood.

Dissolving sugar in water is another physical change. You have made sugary water, but if you heat it up and the water is evaporated, the water and sugar can be completely separated again, and no new substance has been made.

In a chemical change, a new substance is formed and it can never be reversed, or undone.

For example, if you burned a log, a new substance would be made - charcoal, and you could never make it go back to the way it was before.

You can usually tell if a chemical change is taking place because it often produces heat, or changes in colour, or has an odour or smell.

Are the changes below physical or chemical?

• Slicing a tomato		• Tearing paper		• Cooking a cake	
• Defrosting peas		• BBQ steak		• Freezing water	
• Cutting wood		• Scrunching tissues		• Dissolving sugar	
• Frying bacon		• Melting plastic		• Boiling eggs	

Physical or Chemical Change?

Skills:

Conduct experiments, record data, and analyse results.

In this activity, you will conduct three different experiments to see whether a physical change or a chemical change is happening.

What You Need

- baking soda
- vinegar
- plastic bottle (no cap)
- milk
- large coffee mug
- nail
- rock
- measuring cups and spoons

Directions

Experiment 1

Pour ½ cup (120 mL) of vinegar into the plastic bottle. Then pour 1 tablespoon (7.5 g) of baking soda into the bottle. Record your observations in the chart on page 119.

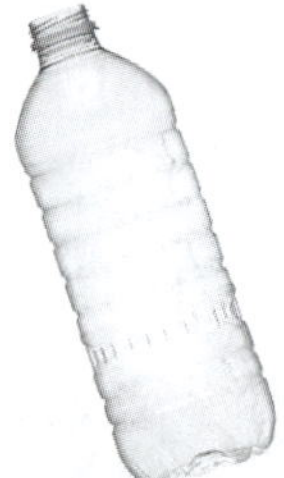

Experiment 2

1. Put 4 teaspoons (20 mL) of vinegar in a large heat-resistant mug.
2. Ask an adult to help you heat up 1 cup (.25 L) of milk on the stove or in the microwave.
3. Add the milk to the vinegar in the mug. Record your observations.

Experiment 3

Scratch your initials into the rock with the nail. Record your observations.

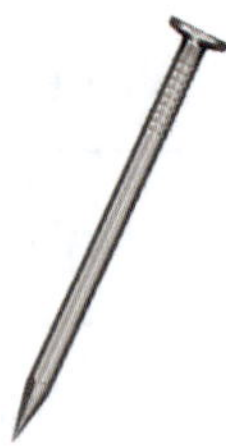

Chemistry

TARGETING SCIENCE YEAR 6 © PASCAL PRESS ISBN: 9781925726558

	How substances changed
Experiment 1	
Experiment 2	
Experiment 3	

What Did You Discover?

1. What happened after you poured the baking soda into the vinegar in Experiment 1?

2. What happened after you poured the hot milk into the vinegar in Experiment 2?

3. What happened after you scratched the rock with the nail in Experiment 3?

4. Which experiments do you think were chemical changes? Which were physical changes? Explain your answer.

Dissolving Salt - A physical or chemical change?

For this investigation you will need:

- 4 tablespoons of cooking salt (or any other kind of salt)
- ½ a cup of water (warm is better)
- A teaspoon for mixing
- A cup to mix in
- Some black or dark cardboard
- A sunny spot
- An eyedropper or pipette

Procedure:

1. Add the salt water to the water in the cup and mix until it has dissolved, or almost completely dissolved. If it won't dissolve fully, don't worry, it might be 'saturated' which is the scientific way to describe when a solution can't dissolve any more solid into a liquid.
2. Lie the black cardboard or paper in the sun, where it will be able to lie still without blowing away. You might need to put some rocks in the corners.
3. Use the dropper or pipette to suck up the salty solution, and then make a pattern or picture on the card by dripping it on carefully.
4. Leave it in the sun until the liquid has evaporated.

Results:

1. What did you find?

____

____

2. Draw what your solution looks like now.

3. Why did this happen?

____

____

4. Was this a physical or chemical change? How do you know?

____

____

____

Chemistry

Physical and Chemical Changes

Skill:

Write a compare-and-contrast essay.

Compare and contrast physical changes and chemical changes. You may look back at the "Physical Properties and Chemical Properties" lesson (page 114) for more information about physical changes. Be sure to include examples of both physical and chemical changes.

Reversible changes in Recycling

Landfill is a huge worldwide problem. Waste from our homes and offices can take years and even centuries to break down, and billions of tonnes of natural resources are required to make new materials.

https://clickv.ie/w/j0gx

Use this QR code to access a video on this topic.

Recycling plastic and glass is possible because the chemical properties allow them to be heated and cooled and yet remain unchanged. However, it's not as simple as melting and re-freezing an ice-block.

Once the products have been melted down, they can then be made into something else by adding new chemicals. In the case of plastics, it doesn't mean that the world can start producing less plastic, but these recycled products can be used instead of products like clothing, outdoor furniture, playground equipment and modified wood, which then reduces the amount of trees that need to be cut down.

Glass can be sorted and melted down with some added raw materials to make new glass.

The paper making process is also reversible. Used paper is pulped, chemicals are added and then it is processed to make paper again.

Have you ever noticed the triangular label that you see on plastic items?

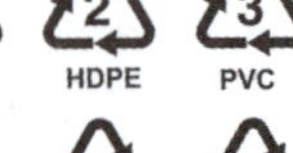

These labels identify the type of plastic the item is made from and is used when plastics are sorted during the first stage of the recycling process.

High density plastics (2) are recycled into things that need to be really durable, like toys. Low density plastics (4) are used for less durable items like food wrapping and plastic bags.

1. Why is it possible to recycle materials such as plastic, glass and paper?

____

2. What is the main difference between recycling glass and recycling plastic?

____

____

Reversible Change - a First Nations Perspective

https://clickv.ie/w/9ygx

Use this QR code to access a video on this topic.

Resin is a plant produced substance that has been used by First Nations Peoples throughout time. Resin, when heated, becomes soft and malleable. Once the source of heat is removed, the resin cools and hardens again, demonstrating a **reversible change** in the state of matter.

Resin can be used as a glue, a waterproofing agent, fuel for torches, and for the repair and strengthening of implements. A wide range of plants exude resin. The type of plant used depends on the vegetation that is available.

In the Murray River region in South Australia, The Ngarrindjeri Peoples mix the resin of the grasstree with sand to join sharp quartz tips to spears. They also find resinous timber to use as a torch during spear fishing trips by canoe at night.

The Yidinji Peoples of far North Queensland mix grasstree resin with beeswax, charcoal, sand or dust, to prepare a mixture to attach stone heads to wooden handles and spear shafts to tips. In the Sydney basin region, The Gadigal Peoples of the Eora Nation used grasstree resin to reinforce the joints of fish hooks and to mend damaged canoes.

All of these uses were made possible because of the reversible properties of resin. It can be heated and cooled repeatedly, which then allows things to be reshaped and repaired.

Irreversible changes result in a change of colour, a release of odour, gas, light or sound or a change in temperature. If resin is overheated, it undergoes an irreversible change, which makes it a lot less useful. Timber with a lot of resin in it burns to make a very bright light with very little smoke. Eventually, after burning for a long time, the change becomes irreversible and the resin becomes brittle and the branch becomes charred.

1. What is one way in which resin is used by indigenous people resulting in a reversible change?

____

____

2. What is one way in which resin is used by indigenous people resulting in an irreversible change?

____

____

Corrosion

Concepts:

The chemical reaction of corrosion causes iron, oxygen, and water to change into rust.

Define It!

barrier: something that prevents or blocks movement from one place to another

corrosion: a chemical wearing away of a material

expose: to be in the open, unprotected

interact: to come together and have an effect on each other

A chemical reaction happens when substances **interact** and their molecules change. There are many different types of chemical reactions. The type of chemical reaction that takes place between substances depends on their chemical properties, or potential to go through a change.

One common type of chemical reaction is called **corrosion**. Rust is a sign of corrosion, which occurs when metal is **exposed** to air and moisture. The chemical reaction of corrosion causes iron, oxygen, and water to change into iron oxide, or rust. However, there are ways to stop metal from corroding. One way is to paint the metal. The paint forms a protective **barrier** between the oxygen and the moisture in the air.

The Golden Gate Bridge is painted to protect its metal from corrosion.

Answer the questions.

1. What is one way to keep metal from corroding?

____

2. When does corrosion occur?

____

3. In the chemical reaction of corrosion, iron, oxygen, and water change into what substance?

____

Chemistry

TARGETING SCIENCE YEAR 6 © PASCAL PRESS ISBN: 9781925726558

Another common chemical reaction is called **combustion**. Combustion occurs when substances combine with oxygen to make new substances and, in the process, produce heat and light. In other words, combustion is burning. Combustion happens when you light a match, burn a candle, or turn on your gas stove.

Combustion needs oxygen in order to take place. Oxygen is one of the main reactants of the chemical reaction. If you tried to light a match in a room with no oxygen, the match would not burn. The other reactant of combustion is usually a type of **fuel**. When the fuel and the oxygen combine, they create carbon dioxide and water. Besides producing the new substances of carbon dioxide and water, the chemical reaction also releases energy. During combustion, energy is released in the form of heat and light, or fire.

Define It!

combustion: the burning of a substance

fuel: a substance such as coal, gas, or oil that can be burned for heat or power

A match produces a flame through the chemical reaction of combustion.

Concepts: The chemical reaction of combustion occurs when substances combine with oxygen to produce heat and light.

Answer the questions.

1. What are the typical reactants of combustion?

____

2. What are the products of combustion?

____

3. What type of energy is released as a result of combustion?

____

TARGETING SCIENCE YEAR 6 © PASCAL PRESS ISBN: 9781925726558

Acid-Base Reactions

Concepts:
Acid-base reactions occur when an acid and a base combine to create salt and water.

Define It!

acid: a chemical with a sour taste that forms a salt when mixed with a base

base: a chemical with a bitter taste that forms a salt when mixed with an acid

neutralise: to cause a chemical to be neither an acid nor a base

Another common chemical reaction is an acid-base reaction. An acid-base reaction is a chemical reaction that occurs between an **acid** and a **base**. An acid is a substance that often has a sour taste. Orange juice and vinegar are acids. A base is a substance that is often slippery and bitter tasting. Household ammonia, soap, and shampoo are all bases. Acids and bases frequently react with one another to make sodium chloride, or salt, and water.

When a person takes an antacid tablet to help with heartburn, he or she is actually starting an acid-base reaction. Heartburn happens when the acid in a person's stomach becomes too strong. Antacid tablets contain a base. When the person with heartburn takes the tablet, the base in the antacid reacts with the acid in the person's stomach. The antacid **neutralises** the stomach acid and gets rid of the heartburn. What's left is water and salt.

Orange juice is an acid.

Soap is a base.

Answer the questions.

1. Name two examples of acids mentioned in the passage. Can you think of any other substances that might be acids?

____

____

2. Name two examples of bases mentioned in the passage. Can you think of any other substances that might be bases?

____

____

Chemistry

Skill:
Interpret information from graphic images.

Look at the pictures showing a candle as it is lit and after it has been blown out. Then answer the questions below.

1. Name a physical property of the unlit candle in picture **1**.

____

2. Name a physical property of the candle that has been blown out in picture **4**.

____

3. What starts the chemical reaction of the wick burning in picture **2**?

____

4. Which product of combustion is visible in picture **3**?

____

5. Which product of combustion is visible in picture **4**?

____

Chemistry

Skill:

Apply content vocabulary.

Select from the vocabulary words to complete the sentences. Then unscramble the shaded letters to decode the secret message.

corrosion	fuel	neutralise	expose
combustion	base	barrier	acid

1. One way to ___ ___ [___] ___ ___ ___ [___] ___ ___ ___ stomach ___ ___ ___ ___ is to take an antacid tablet.

2. Burning a candle is an example of the chemical reaction of ___ ___ ___ [___] ___ ___ ___ ___ ___ ___.

3. ___ ___ ___ ___ ___ [___] ___ ___ ___ is a type of chemical reaction that can produce rust.

4. One of the products of an acid-[___] ___ ___ ___ reaction is salt.

5. One way to keep metal from rusting is to form a protective [___] ___ ___ ___ ___ [___] ___ by painting it.

When an acid and a base are mixed, ___ ___ ___ ___ ___ ___ ___ ___ can sometimes form.

TARGETING SCIENCE YEAR 6 © PASCAL PRESS ISBN: 9781925726558

Skill:

Label images that represent scientific concepts.

When methane gas burns, it reacts with oxygen to form water and carbon dioxide. The diagram below shows how the molecules re-form to make new combinations. Label the *products* and the *reactants*. Then circle the symbol that shows where a chemical reaction is taking place.

C = carbon

H = hydrogen

O = oxygen

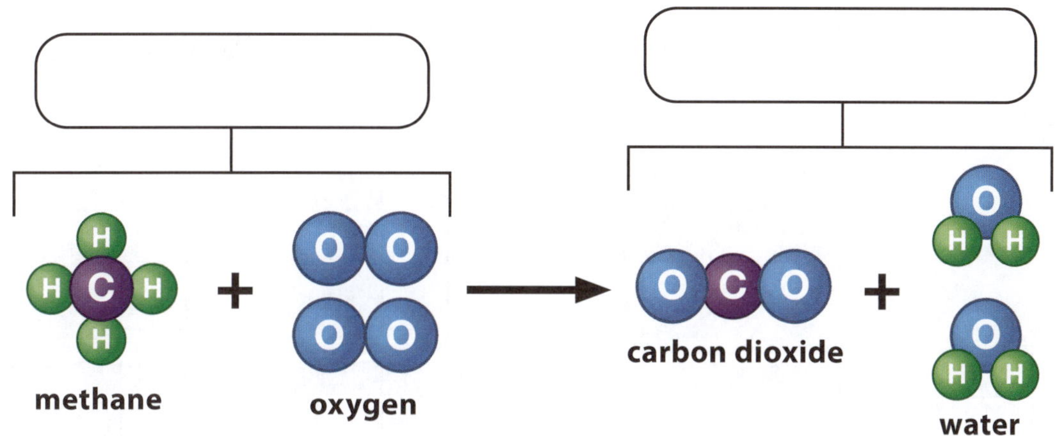

Describe what is happening to the molecules in the diagram. Use the term *conservation of mass* in your answer.

____

____

____

____

____

____

____

Vocabulary Practice

Skill:

Apply content vocabulary.

Select from the list of vocabulary words to complete the crossword puzzle.

conservation of mass	chemical change	physics	bond	ignite
chemical property	molecular	potential	product	reactant

Across

6. the force that holds together the particles of a molecule
7. a substance that changes during a chemical reaction
8. a change in which a new substance is formed

Down

1. the potential of a substance to change into a different substance
2. a new substance formed during a chemical reaction
3. to catch fire
4. relating to molecules
5. the science of energy and matter

TARGETING SCIENCE YEAR 6 © PASCAL PRESS ISBN: 9781925726558

What Is Chemical Energy?

Concepts:

Chemical energy is energy stored in the chemical bonds of molecules.

Chemical energy is a type of potential energy.

Define It!

bond: the force by which atoms are bound together in a molecule

chemical energy: energy that is stored in the chemical bonds of molecules

There are many forms of energy. **Chemical energy** is energy that is stored in the chemical **bonds** of molecules. It exists in the particles that make up food, fuel, and other substances. The food that you eat contains chemical energy, which you can then use to help you walk, jump, or move. The chemical energy stored in batteries is used to power electrical devices. And the chemical energy in wood, gas, and other fuels can be used to warm our homes.

Chemical energy is a type of potential energy, or energy that is stored due to an object's position. For example, a bike that is on top of a hill has potential energy due to its position. In the case of chemical energy, the potential energy is due to the positions of the molecules within a substance, such as food for fuel.

These objects contain stored chemical energy.

Complete the sentences.

1. The chemical energy that we use to move our bodies comes from ____________________.

2. Energy is stored in the chemical ____________________ of a substance's molecules.

Chemistry

Chemical Reactions

Concept:

Chemical energy is released and converted into other forms of energy during a chemical reaction.

Define It!

chemical reaction: a process in which substances react to form new substances

digest: to break down food into substances that can be used by the body

Chemical energy is stored in the bonds between the molecules of a substance. For example, sugar is made up of carbon, oxygen, and hydrogen atoms held together by chemical bonds. These atoms don't just stick together—energy is required to keep them in place. That energy is chemical energy. In order for us to use chemical energy to do work, however, it must be released in a **chemical reaction**.

During a chemical reaction, the bonds that hold molecules together are broken, transforming chemical potential energy into other forms of energy. This transformation results in a whole new substance being formed. For example, when our bodies **digest** sugar, the chemical bonds of the sugar molecules are broken, changing the sugar into carbon dioxide and water. This chemical reaction results in chemical energy being released in the form of kinetic energy. The kinetic energy then allows us to move our bodies.

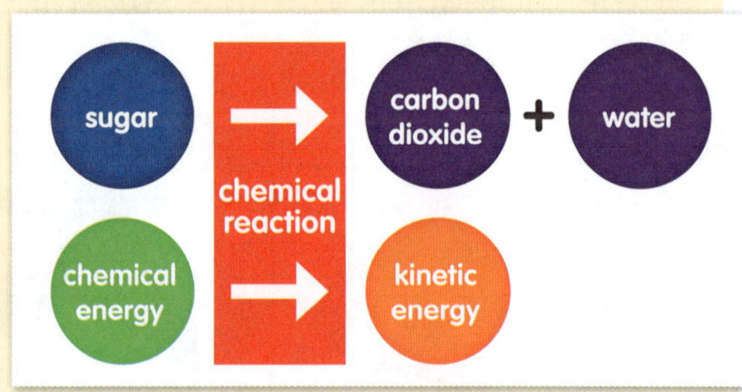

Answer the questions.

1. During digestion, what new substances are formed from sugar? ______________________

2. What holds the atoms of a sugar molecule together? ______________________

3. What must happen in order for chemical energy to be released so that we can do work? ______________________

Chemistry

TARGETING SCIENCE YEAR 6 © PASCAL PRESS ISBN: 9781925726558

Exothermic Reactions

Concept: An exothermic reaction is a chemical reaction in which heat is generated.

Define It!

exothermic reaction: a chemical reaction in which heat is generated

product: a new substance that is formed during a chemical reaction

A chemical reaction changes chemical energy into other forms of energy. During many chemical reactions, heat is also released in the process. When this happens, it is called an **exothermic reaction**. In an exothermic reaction, heat is a **product** of the chemical reaction.

An example of an exothermic reaction is when we use petrol to drive our cars. When you start a car, its engine breaks down the chemicals in petrol. As the chemical bonds holding the petrol together are broken, chemical energy changes into mechanical energy that is used to move the car. The release of the chemical energy also generates heat. That's why the hood of a car feels hot after you've been driving.

Write *true* or *false*.

1. An exothermic reaction is not a chemical reaction. __________
2. The chemical energy of petrol converts into mechanical energy when you start a car. __________
3. An exothermic reaction generates heat. __________
4. Chemical energy changes into other forms of energy in a chemical reaction. __________

Match Up

Skill:

Label images that represent scientific concepts.

A match produces a flame through a chemical reaction called *combustion*. During combustion, chemicals in the match combine with oxygen in the air to make new substances and, in the process, produce light energy and heat.

Look at the three images below. Circle where you think the chemicals are stored in the unused match. Label the *heat and light* created by the chemical reaction. Finally, draw a square around the new substance created.

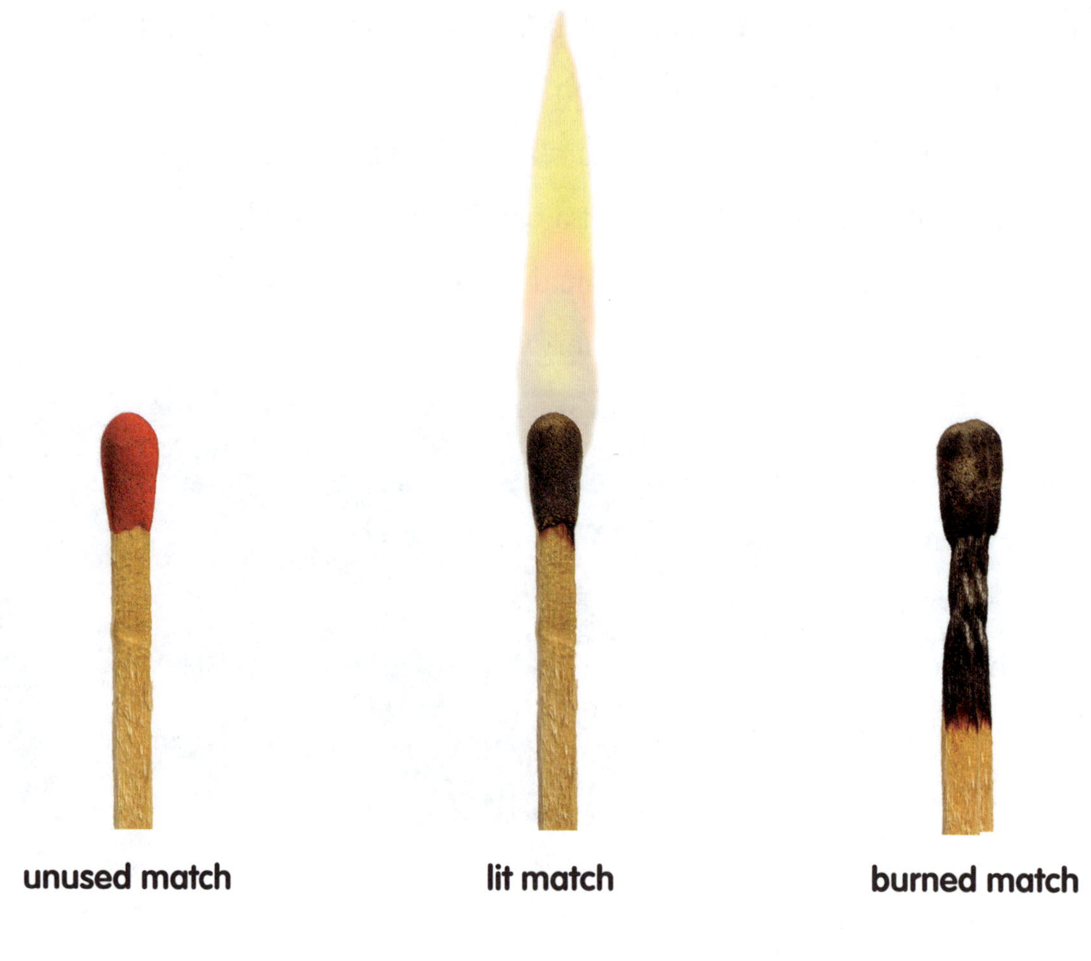

unused match **lit match** **burned match**

Explain why lighting a match is an exothermic reaction.

____

____

____

____

TARGETING SCIENCE YEAR 6 © PASCAL PRESS ISBN: 9781925726558

Skill: Apply content vocabulary.

Use the vocabulary words to complete the sentences. Then unscramble the shaded letters to decode the secret message.

chemical energy	chemical reaction	digest
exothermic reaction	bonds	product

1. In a ___ ___ ___ ___ ___ ___ ___ ___ ___ ___ ___ ___ ___ ___ ___ ___, substances react to form new substances.

2. ___ ___ ___ ___ ___ ___ ___ ___ ___ ___ ___ ___ ___ ___ is contained in the ___ ___ ___ ___ ___ between the molecules of a substance.

3. When we ___ ___ ___ ___ ___ ___ our food, we convert its chemical energy into other forms of energy.

4. An ___ ___ ___ ___ ___ ___ ___ ___ ___ ___ ___ ___ ___ ___ ___ ___ ___ ___ is a reaction in which heat is a ___ ___ ___ ___ ___ ___ ___.

Lighting a match is a type of chemical reaction called ___ ___ ___ ___ ___ ___ ___ ___ ___ ___.

Chemistry

Steel Reaction

Skills:

Conduct experiments and draw conclusions about results.

In this exothermic chemical reaction, you will see what happens when you remove the protective coating of steel wool by soaking it in vinegar.

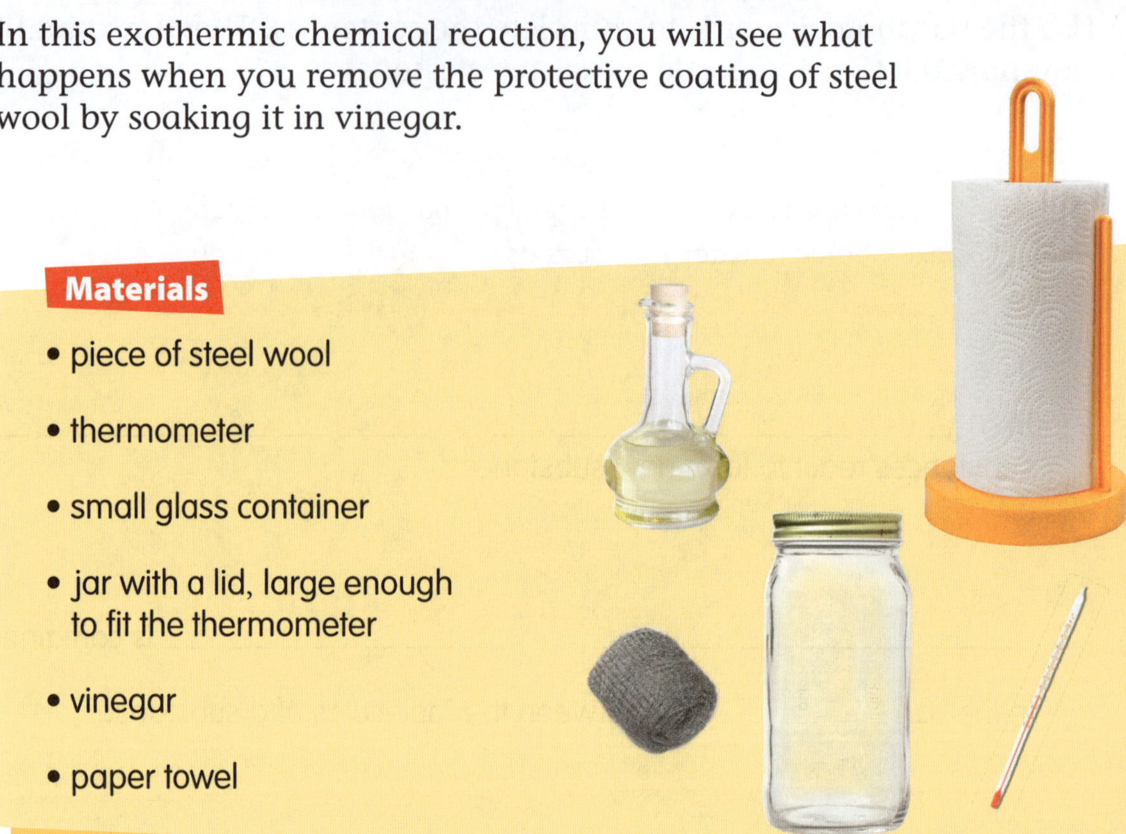

Materials

- piece of steel wool
- thermometer
- small glass container
- jar with a lid, large enough to fit the thermometer
- vinegar
- paper towel

Directions

1. Place the thermometer in the jar and close the lid. Allow 5 minutes for the thermometer to read the temperature inside the jar.
2. Open the lid and read the thermometer. Record the temperature on page 137.
3. Pour some vinegar into the glass container. Add the piece of steel wool and let it soak for 1 minute.
4. Squeeze the excess vinegar from the steel wool, and then wrap it around the bulb of the thermometer.
5. Place the wrapped thermometer in the jar and close the lid.
6. Wait for 5 minutes. On page 137 under "Observations," record any changes you observe from when you first placed the wrapped thermometer in the jar.
7. Open the lid. Remove the steel wool from the thermometer and read and record the temperature.
8. Leave the steel wool out on a paper towel for 2 days. Record any changes you observe.

TARGETING SCIENCE YEAR 6 © PASCAL PRESS ISBN: 9781925726558

	Degrees Celsius (°C)
Temperature 1 (empty sealed jar)	
Temperature 2 (after reaction)	

Observations

During the reaction in the sealed jar:

____

____

Two days after the reaction:

____

____

What Did You Discover?

1. How can you tell that this is an exothermic reaction?

   ____

   ____

   ____

2. What new substance was created from the chemical reaction of the vinegar with the steel wool? ____________________

Chemistry

Energy Conversion

Skill:

Organise text-based information.

All forms of energy—chemical, mechanical, electrical, radiant, thermal, and sound—can be transformed into other forms of energy. Read the description of the chemical reactions that take place when you set off a firework. Then select the correct forms of energy used in the reactions and the order in which they take place.

> To set off a firework, first you place the firework, a shell containing a mixture of chemicals, in a safe place. Then you light the fuse and the firework heats up, blasting into the sky. Soon it explodes in a shower of light! A few moments later, a resounding BOOM rocks the crowd of delighted onlookers.

- ☐ electrical energy to mechanical, chemical, and radiant energy
- ☐ mechanical energy to electrical, sound, and radiant energy
- ☐ chemical energy to thermal, mechanical, radiant, and sound energy
- ☐ radiant energy to electrical, thermal, and chemical energy

TARGETING SCIENCE YEAR 6 © PASCAL PRESS ISBN: 9781925726558

Page 2

1 absorb water from the soil; 2 roots, stems

Page 3

1 chlorophyll, in the chloroplasts in the leaves; 2 stomata, on the undersides of leaves

Page 4

1 false; 2 true; 3 true; 4 false

Page 5

1 (top to bottom) sunlight, oxygen, water; 2 (left to right) carbon dioxide, water

3 The plant absorbs water through its roots. Chlorophyll allows plants to absorb sunlight, and CO2 enters the plant through its stomata. Plants get rid of oxygen and water through their stomata as well.

Page 6

1 vascular, nonvascular; 2 chlorophyll; 3 stomata; 4 photosynthesis; 5 chloroplast; 6 absorb; message: star moss

Page 7

1 The plant covered with jelly did not grow as much as the plant without it.

2 It blocked carbon dioxide from entering the plant.

Page 8

1 It grew curved along the maze towards the light, to get as much sunlight as possible.

2 The plant would have grown to the side.

3 The plant likely would have died.

Page 9

Answers will vary, but should tell a story that shows an understanding of how sunlight, carbon dioxide and water are equally important.

Page 10

1 The ones where the animals live and/or reproduce in the pond.

2 Over time, they might die out. This is because the habitat is gradually declining or being destroyed.

Page 11

Beach: oil covering any plants on beach will slow their growth, animals that live in shore severely impacted and may die if not rescued, serious levels of pollution damage environment.

Native forest: plants cut down and cleared; habitat loss for animals that live in forest; rocks, soil etc cleared and replaced by built environment.

Page 12

True: coral grows in warmer waters; coral ejects algae from its body when stressed; coral bleaching only happens to stressed coral; you can see the GBR from space; coral is living; the GBR is made up of 3000 smaller reefs

False: coral is a plant; coral is not affected by the height of the water above it; coral moves from place to place

Page 13

1 What is the effect on the growth of mould of placing bread in different positions?

2 changed variable - positioning; observe - amount of mould; keep the same - type of bread, amount of water on bread, length of time

4 least mould in the fridge

5 store bread in fridge or freezer

Page 17

1 24 hours; 2 anticlockwise; 3 the North and South Poles

Page 18

1 false; 2 true; 3 true; 4 false

Page 19

1 We would have 6 months of daylight and 6 months of darkness.

2 One side of the planet would be very hot, while the other would be very cold.

3 Plant and animal life that could not adapt would perish.

Page 20

Barrow, St Petersburg, Shanghai, Bogota

Page 21

1 answers will vary; 2 no; 3 answers will vary; 4 no; 5 The sun was lower in the sky in the morning and higher in the sky in the afternoon.

Page 22

1 night; 2 sunrise, sunset; 3 noon

Page 23

1 three; 2 (west to east) 1 ½ hours, ½ hour; 3 Eastern Standard Time; 4 11 am; 5 8:30 am

Page 24

1 gravity; 2 everything would float off into space; 3 mass and distance; 4 affect on tides; 5 less; 6 lesser

Page 26

1 When the Northern Hemisphere is titled towards the Sun.

2 The Earth's axis is tilted towards the Sun, and therefore the Sun's rays have a greater intensity.

3 summer, winter

Page 27

1 true; 2 false; 3 false; 4 false

Page 28

1 it is much closer to Earth than any other star; 2 average; 3 you could fit 1.3 million Earths inside the Sun

Page 29

1 150 million km; 2 271,000 astronomical units; 3 4.2 light years; 4 9.46 trillion km

Page 30

1 100 astronomical units; 2 5 astronomical units; 3 150 million km; 4 10,000

Page 32

1 18 sheets, 541,968,048 km; 2 148 sheets, 4,456,181,726 km; 3 1,441,589,200 km; 4 153,532 metres

Page 33

Answers may vary, but should show an understanding of how far away Proxima Centauri is from Earth in light years.

Page 35

1 red, yellow, white or blue

2 our sun is white, not yellow, and it is average size

Page 37

1 B; 2 A

Page 38

1 summer; 2 autumn; 3 summer

Page 39

1 classify, dwarf star; 2 constellations, mythical figures; 3 position; 4 misleading; 5 galaxy; message: Gemini

Page 43

1 true; 2 true; 3 false; 4 true

Page 44

1 Longer, because the sun hits at a greater angle.

2 Far North Queensland, because the sun hits at a greater angle.

Page 45

Landscape: snow reflects the sun's energy.

Weather: a dry climate means there are few clouds to keep heat close to the ground. Wind blows away surface heat.

Page 46

1 July, August, September; 2 January; 3 South Pole average temperatures are lower.

Page 47

1 climate; 2 equator; 3 curvature; 4 atmosphere; 5 landscape; message: arctic

Page 49

1 likely more snow in Buffalo; 2 likely warmer during precipitation; 3 precipitation less likely at lower temperatures

Page 50

1 six; 2 tropical and cool temperate; 3 subtropical and cool temperate; 4 arid

Page 51

1 It contains the gases we need to breathe. It keeps temperatures on Earth even. It allows for water to exist as a liquid.

2 The atmosphere traps the sun's heat to warm the planet. The atmosphere also keeps out harmful rays from the sun.

Page 52

1 true; 2 false; 3 false; 4 true

Page 53

1 methane; 2 as a waste product mostly through burping; 3 they produce less gas, they take less water to raise, it protects other food sources

Page 54

1 producing electricity; 2 11.6 %; 3 public transport, bike, walk, hybrid cars

Page 55

1 thrive; 2 greenhouse gases; 3 fossil fuels, atmosphere; 4 livestock; 5 emit; 6 environment; message: greenhouse effect

Page 57

1 It was warmer than room temperature.

2 It was warmer than Aquarium A and much warmer than room temperature.

3 It increases the temperature on our planet.

Page 58

1 volcanic eruptions, asteroids; 2 dramatic shifts in temperatures, sea levels and ocean currents

Page 59

1 true; 2 true; 3 false

Page 60

1 greenhouse, fossil; 2 drought, temperatures

Page 61

1 increasing; 2 2005: 38 billion, 1990: 31 billion; 3 carbon dioxide; 4 6 billion metric tons

Page 62

1 climate change; 2 greenhouse gases; 3 fossil fuels; 4 glaciers; 5 uninhabitable; 6 extinction; message: greenhouse effect

Page 64

1 no; 2 yes; 3 South Pole

Page 65

1 stronger storms, rising sea level, more evaporation; 2 warmer atmosphere, melting snow and ice, more evaporation; 3 more evaporation

TARGETING SCIENCE YEAR 6 © PASCAL PRESS ISBN: 9781925726558

Page 66

(left to right) heat, air pressure, wind, precipitation

Page 67

Cold air is heavier and applies more pressure, so it sinks. Warm air is lighter and under less pressure, so it rises.

Page 68

(left to right) precipitation, solar energy, condensation, evaporation

Page 69

The wind reverses direction because the warm air over the ocean rises and the cooler air from the land flows in to take its place.

Page 71

1 The lit match heated the air causing it to expand and rise, just as solar energy does to air near the Earth's surface.

2 The greater pressure outside the bottle forced the egg down into the bottle.

3 The pressure was not greater inside the bottle, so nothing forced the egg out.

4 Blowing into the bottle increased the pressure inside the bottle so that it was greater than the pressure outside the bottle. This pushed the egg out.

Page 72

Answers will vary but should show understanding of how solar energy controls temperature, wind and precipitation, and that without solar energy there would be no weather on Earth.

Page 75

Series circuit advantages: you know if there is a break in the circuit

Series circuit disadvantages: if one breaks, whole thing doesn't work, the more bulbs you add, the dimmer the lights become

Parallel circuit advantages: the circuit will still work even if one path fails, the lights don't get dimmer if you add more of them

Parallel circuit disadvantages: you don't know if there is a break in the circuit

Page 76

Conductors: metal cutlery, keys, metal pen, magnet, metal pencil tin, biscuit tin

Insulators: glass, ceramic cup, wooden desk, pencil, plastic pen, book, wooden chair

Page 77

1 false; 2 true

Page 78

1 resistor; 2 circuit

Page 79

1 false; 2 true; 3 true

Page 80

switch (left) filaments (right)

When the toast pops up, the electric current stops. This is because the switch gets turned off, which breaks the circuit.

Page 81

The lever on the toaster moves a switch which closes the circuit. Electric current flows through the circuit and causes the filament, a resistor, to heat up. The heat transfers to the bread in the toaster and causes the bread to toast.

Page 82

1 electric current; 2 circuit; 3 switch; 4 conductor; 5 insulator; 6 filaments; 7 electron

Page 83

1 The energy produced by the movement of electrons between atoms.

2 Static electricity is an electric charge that builds up on an object that has gained or lost electrons. It is temporary and difficult to control. Electric current can be made to flow through wires and is easier to control.

Page 85

1 I heard a snap and felt a shock.

2 I heard a snap, saw a spark, and felt a stronger shock. There was a spark this time and the shock was stronger.

3 I saw a bright spark between my finger and the nail. The spark was brighter than when I touched the pie pan the second time.

4 rubbing the plate with the wool cloth

Page 87

1 hydroelectricity; 2 turbine; 3 digital; 4 resistor; 5 filament; 6 segment; 7 display; 8 circuit

Page 88

3 The electromagnet picks up the paper clips.

Page 89

7 The larger the number of coils, the stronger the electromagnet became.

Page 90

(left to right and top to bottom)

no, water is a conductor; yes, no cables to hit; no, not secure; no, lightning may strike tree; no, need an expert; yes, water a conductor; no, it might fall in the bathtub; yes, water can damage computer; no, might hit a cable; yes, so no electricity flows; yes, could be electrocuted; no, could be electrocuted

Page 91

1 electrical; 2 mechanical; 3 potential; 4 chemical

Page 92

1 motion, sound; 2 light, sound; 3 light, heat; 4 light, sound; 5 sound; 6 heat, light

Answer Key

Page 93

Kinetic energy is transferred from the cue to the ball. Then, when the ball hits another ball, it is transferred to the second ball.

Page 94

1 true; 2 false; 3 false

Page 95

(left hand side) potential, potential, potential

(right hand side) kinetic, kinetic

Page 97

1 wind turbines; 2 water falling over a dam

Page 98

1 false; 2 true; 3 false; 4 true

Page 99

We hear the popcorn making a popping sound when it changes from a kernel to a white puff.

Page 100

Conduction through physical contact, radiation through energy waves that move through matter or empty space, convection through the movement of a liquid or a gas.

Page 101

(left to right) conduction, convection, radiation

The air is warmed by convection through the smoke. The marshmallow is toasted by radiation coming off the barbeque. The patty is cooked by conduction where it touches the barbeque grill.

Page 102

1 radiation; 2 generate; 3 heat, thermal energy; 4 temperature; 5 internal; 6 conduction; message: electromagnetic

Page 104

1 potential; 2 kinetic; 3 The car goes further and faster because more potential energy has been built up, which is then converted to more kinetic energy.

Page 105

1 vibrations; 2 electron; 3 transform; 4 convert; 5 energy; 6 incline; 7 kinetic energy; 8 condition

Page 106

1 organic; 2 structure; 3 physical

Page 107

Fruit punch: flavouring - solute, water - solvent

Sparkling water: water - solvent, CO_2 - solute

Chocolate milk: milk - solvent, sugar - solute, cocoa - solute

Page 108

1 sugar; 2 carbon dioxide; 3 oxygen

Page 109

Rocks 1 - easiest to separate, can just pick them apart by hand.

Sand 2 - harder to separate because the particles are very small.

Smoothie 3 - hardest to separate because the ingredients are blended together.

Page 110

1 mixture; 2 solute, solvent; 3 soluble; 4 solution; 5 organic; 6 solubility, dissolve; message: alloys

Page 112

Cup 1 - salt dissolved, sunlight evaporates water

Cup 2 - sand slowly sank, coffee filter

Cup 3 - gravel quickly sank, strainer

Cup 4 - iron filings sank, magnet

1 The salt water is a solution, because the salt blended evenly throughout the water.

2 Some of the water disappeared, leaving a salt rim behind.

3 Leave the water out in a warm place for a long time so that it evaporates, leaving the salt behind. Or boil the water to evaporate it, leaving the salt behind.

4 The coffee filter was best for the sand because it could catch the tiny pieces of rock and shell. The strainer was best for the gravel, because the pieces were larger and heavier. The magnet was best for the iron filings because iron is attracted to magnets.

Page 114

1 false; 2 true; 3 true; 4 false

Page 115

1 iron and oxygen, iron oxide (rust)

2 In a physical change, no new substance is made. In a chemical change, a new substance is created.

Page 116

1 4; 2 4;

3 Yes, the number of oxygen particles is the same because mass has not been or destroyed. It was only rearranged.

Page 117

P	P	C
P	C	P
P	P	P
C	C	C

TARGETING SCIENCE YEAR 6 © PASCAL PRESS ISBN: 9781925726558

Page 119

Exp 1 vinegar bubbled up; Exp 2 milk curdled and clumped together; Exp 3 rock had scratches on it

1 The baking soda dissolved into the vinegar and the vinegar started bubbling.

2 The milk started to curdle and clumped together. It became a solid.

3 The rock had scratches on it.

4 Experiments 1 and 2 were chemical changes because they created new substances—bubbles and curdled milk. Experiment 3 was a physical change because the rock was still a rock, it just had scratches on it.

Page 120

1 The water was gone and the salt was left behind, wherever the drips were.

3 The water had evaporated but the salt did not.

4 Physical. Because the substances could go back to their original forms.

Page 121

Answers will vary but must demonstrate an understanding of the basic principles of physical properties and chemical properties, as well as the law of conservation of mass. Answer should also include the key difference between physical and chemical changes—that physical changes do not change the substances themselves, while chemical changes result in new substances being formed.

Page 122

1 Their chemical properties allow them to be heated and cooled and yet remain unchanged.

2 Recycled plastics can be used instead of other products, recycled glass can be made into new glass.

Page 123

1 Adding heat and then allowing it to cool again.

2 By overheating it.

Page 124

1 paint the metal; 2 when metal is exposed to air and mositure; 3 iron oxide (rust)

Page 125

1 oxygen and a fuel; 2 CO2 and water; heat and light

Page 126

1 orange juice and vinegar, answers will vary—example: lemon juice and acid rain

2 soap and shampoo, answers will vary—example: cleaning products and toothpaste

Page 127

1 solid wax; 2 melted wax; 3 the flame from the match; 4 fire; 5 smoke

Page 128

1 neutralise, acid; 2 combustion; 3 corrosion; 4 base; 5 barrier; message: bubbles

Page 129

reactants (left), products(right)

The methane and oxygen molecules recombine into carbon dioxide and water molecules. The mass of the molecules is balanced when they re-form. This means there is conservation of mass in the chemical reaction.

Page 130

1 chemical property; 2 product; 3 ignite; 4 molecular; 5 physics; 6 bond; 7 reactant; 8 chemical change

Page 131

1 food; 2 bonds

Page 132

1 CO2 and water; 2 chemical energy; 3 a chemical reaction

Page 133

1 false; 2 true; 3 true; 4 true

Page 134

chemicals in red tip of unburnt match; heat and light in the flame; new substance in the burned match

As chemical energy is changed into light energy, it generates heat as a product

Page 135

1 chemical reaction; 2 chemical energy, bonds; 3 digest; 4 exothermic reaction, product; message: combustion

Page 137

During the reaction in the sealed jar: The glass of the jar fogged up. The thermometer reading rose.

Two days after the reaction: The steel of the wool began to rust. It darkened in colour as time passed.

1 The temperature rose in the jar, showing that heat was produced from the reaction.

2 rust

Page 138

chemical energy to thermal, mechanical, radiant, and sound energy